disciples
who will last

Disciples Who Will Last
Copyright © Tim Hawkins 2007

Published by The Good Book Company
Elm House, 37 Elm Road, New Malden, Surrey KT3 3HB, UK
Telephone: 0845 225 0880; International: +44 (0) 208 942 0880
email: admin@thegoodbook.co.uk
Websites:
UK: www.thegoodbook.co.uk
USA & Canada: www.thegoodbook.com
Australia: www.thegoodbook.com.au

Hawkins Ministry Resources
42 York Road, Kellyville. N.S.W. 2155 Australia
Phone: (+61 2) 9629 6595
Fax: (+61 2) 9629 6595
E-mail: info@hawkinsministry.com
Website: www.hawkinsministry.com

ISBN: 9781906334628

Cover design by Steve Devane

Printed in the UK by CPI Bookmarque, Croydon

Thanks heaps...

To Jesus Christ. Without you, not only would there be no book, but I would have no life. You have taken me to The Father, and filled me with your Spirit. Without you, I can do nothing.

To my wife, Karen. Without you, I could not do this ministry. I deeply appreciate the way you put up with me as I wrote each page. You've made lots of helpful comments and timely corrections to what I have written. I love you!

To my daughter Carly, and my son Joshua. The youth ministry "out there" means nothing to me compared with the joy of bringing you two through to Christian adulthood. Thanks for putting up with me as your dad.

To some very special people who helped me finish this book. A number of friends from St. Paul's Castle Hill took the time to read through my manuscript – and came back to me with all sorts of helpful suggestions. This book is so much better because of you! So thank you to:

Luke Davie, Laura Free, Lauren Gardiner, Gavan Lee, James Murray, Caitlin Page, Mark Pullen, Tim van Rees, Sarah Seminara and Peter Tuck

To the many gifted Bible teachers who have sown into my life over the decades. I have been blessed over the years by being taught God's word faithfully by a myriad of people – many of you would barely know that I exist. Thank you for what you have taught me. This book is a result of your faithfulness.

To the students and leaders at *Crossfire* in sunny downtown Castle Hill. Thank you for allowing me to take you on the exciting journey of having your life turned around by Jesus. I love hanging out with you guys and I know God will use you to change this world.

I have taken great care to give due credit to the number of individuals who have impacted my life and ministry. After over three decades in ministry, it is possible that I have inadvertently included material which has not been properly acknowledged. If this has happened, please contact the publisher so that this can be rectified in future editions.

I want to include everyone!

I want everyone to feel that they are included in this book. This can be a little difficult with the limitations of the English language. Historically, the male pronouns "he", "his", "him", (and their derivations) have been used to include people of both genders.

However, not everyone feels included these days by following this tradition. I have avoided the perfectly correct, but cumbersome alternative of always delineating "he/she", "him/her" etc. To try and include everyone, I have opted for the grammatically incorrect, but inclusive "they", "their", "them" etc. I hope that you feel included, and that you do not cringe too much with the damage I have done to the English language!

Contents

Section 1: The Vision for Discipling

Section 2: Getting Disciples Started

Section 3: Getting Disciples Growing

Section 4: Being a Discipleship Leader

Section 5: The Missing Links of Discipling

The Vision for Discipling

SECTION 1

Chapter 1
Why building disciples matters!

Okay – you've picked up this book – you've started to read. You're a busy person – you've got plenty to do – and everyone knows you don't need **yet another** church programme to implement! But something within you is telling you that building *disciples who will last* **really matters!**

The question that has bee most asked of me over the thirty years I have spent in full-time local-church youth ministry is this: *"How do you turn new believers into lasting disciples?"*

Let's look at some of the reasons as to **why** this is such a crucial issue!

1. It deals with the "back door" problem

Fred, the new fired-up youth pastor, was running some great outreach programmes at his church. Cutting-edge stuff. Reaching out into his community and attracting kids with some outrageous activities. The rest of the church looked on with pride as they saw the marvellous things that their youth ministry was pioneering. The front door of the youth group had been flung open wide – and lots of new kids were flocking in. Attendance was up; involvement was up; enthusiasm was up. This was a sure sign of God's revival!

George and Joe were two of those new kids. They were in Year 10 at the local high school. They had never shown much interest in Christianity before. In fact, they had wandered along to the church youth group a few years ago, and their behaviour was so bad that they had been politely asked to leave! But things were different now. Fred was a scintillating youth pastor – the youth programmes were upbeat and cutting edge – and George and Joe were happy to commit themselves every week.

Six months later, George and Joe were nowhere to be seen. They just stopped coming. No real reason. No big disasters. They liked Fred; they liked the programme; they seemed to be making friends. But for some reason, they just stopped coming. They hadn't migrated to the large church down the road, and they hadn't given up on Christianity to sacrifice live chickens at midnight to Satan. They just stopped coming. Still agreeing with everything they had learnt about Jesus. But no longer keen enough to keep at it. The big revival that was sparked through Fred's fired-up programme now seems just a distant memory. It was fun while it lasted, but the truth of the matter is – it simply didn't last.

Fred might have done lots of good things with his emphasis on outreach. But at this stage, he has not been able to produce *disciples who will last*. Sound familiar?

Sometimes new people stay for two weeks or two years, but we all know the problem. We might have lots of new converts walking in through the front door, but in so many churches, there is a constant trickle leaving via the back door. Sometimes we're just not sure what to do to help new believers become life-long disciples.

2. It reflects the heart of Jesus

This book is not just about "closing the back door so we can increase attendance numbers at our church or youth group"! There are far bigger issues at stake here. Is there a way that we can share the very heart of Jesus when he says:

> **John 6:39** *"And this is the will of him who sent me, that I shall lose none of all that he has given me, but raise them up at the last day."*

Imagine we could have that as our goal as well – that we would "lose none of all that God has given us"! Wouldn't it be great if our hearts and souls could be poured into achieving this mighty aim? Building *disciples who will last* is not just about increasing attendance numbers – it is about taking Christ-like care of those who have said "yes" to Jesus, that we might not *lose* one of them! Building disciples who will last is very much about caring deeply for every precious soul whom God has placed in our care.

You know how keen Jesus is to make sure that no one gets lost!

> **Luke 15:4-7** *"Suppose one of you has a hundred sheep and loses one of them. Does he not leave the ninety-nine in the open country and go after the lost sheep until he finds it? And when he finds it, he joyfully puts it on his shoulders and goes home. Then he calls his friends and neighbours together and says, 'Rejoice with me; I have found my lost sheep.' I tell you that in the same way there will be more rejoicing in heaven over one sinner who repents than over ninety-nine righteous persons who do not need to repent."*

If it's worth risking your life to save your lost sheep and bring them back to the fold, then it's also worth risking your life to look after them to make sure that they don't go wandering off again! By growing *disciples who will last*, we are aiming to make sure that *no-one gets lost along the way!*

3. It grows believers to maturity

When we come to Christ, we are like little babies.[1] But God doesn't want us to merely "drink from the baby's spiritual bottle" for the rest of our lives. He has a plan for each one of us. God wants us all to grow to be *just like Jesus.* That's certainly the goal that I am striving to achieve for myself – that I will become *less and less* like the sinful man I used to be, and *more and more* like the sinless Jesus whom I follow. When we throw our weight into developing *disciples who will last,* we are aiming to achieve for each person **the exact same thing** that God wants to achieve for them. *(Does this sound like a ministry worth pouring effort into?)*

When Jesus ministers to people, he always has an end result in mind. We looked at this verse a moment ago. But notice how it **finishes**:

> **John 6:39** *"And this is the will of him who sent me, that I shall lose none of all that he has given me, **but raise them up at the last day**."*

And the reason that Jesus does not want to lose one disciple? His goal for every believer is that he will "*raise them up at the last day*". He emphasises this in the very next verse:

---

1. 1 Peter 2:2

John 6:40 *"For my Father's will is that everyone who looks to the Son and believes in him shall have eternal life, and I will raise him up at the last day."*

Jesus wants to achieve the Father's will – that everyone who trusts in God's Son **shall have eternal life**. That is, they will stick it out to the end. Jesus is not just focusing on "a decision for one day" – but he is emphasising "perseverance for eternity". That is also meant to be our emphasis in producing disciples who will last. We want to be able to say with Paul:

Philippians 1:6 *"that he who began a good work in you will carry it on to completion until the day of Christ Jesus."*

That is God's aim for every disciple. Paul knows this, which is why he works so hard to achieve it.

Colossians 1:28-29 *"We proclaim him, admonishing and teaching everyone with all wisdom, so that we may present everyone perfect in Christ. To this end I labour, struggling with all his energy, which so powerfully works in me."*

What is it that Paul is labouring at – struggling with all his energy to achieve? To *"present everyone perfect [or complete] in Christ"*. The Bible's aim is that every believer keeps becoming mature in Christ – to be less like our sinful selves, and more like the master whom we serve.

Training *disciples who will last* achieves this!

4. It's God's strategy to grow his church

When Paul writes to the Ephesians, he talks about this same maturity as achieving *"the fullness of Christ"*:

> **Ephesians 4:13** *"until we all reach unity in the faith and in the knowledge of the Son of God and become mature, attaining to the whole measure of the fullness of Christ."*

And why does this maturity in Christ matter so much?

> **Ephesians 4:14** *"Then we will no longer be infants, tossed back and forth by the waves, and blown here and there by every wind of teaching and by the cunning and craftiness of men in their deceitful scheming."*

So what will be the result of not being shaken by wrong teaching, but remaining firm in Christ's word?

> **Ephesians 4:15-16** *"Instead, speaking the truth in love, we will in all things grow up into him who is the Head, that is, Christ. From him the whole body, joined and held together by every supporting ligament, grows and builds itself up in love, as each part does its work."*

Here's discipleship in a nutshell. **It is God's plan to grow his church!** Let's follow through again God's plan for growth that Paul has just outlined in Ephesians Chapter 4:

a) *We aim to grow every disciple to become mature in Christ (v 13)...*

b) *So that we will not be shaken – but hold true to the teachings of Christ (v 14)...*

c) *So that we will grow in truth and love to be more like Jesus (v 15)...*

d) *And that way the whole of the church grows! (v 16)*

So growing *disciples who will last* is not just about making our individual church programmes better, or even just looking after each individual Christian. **One of the reasons we aim to grow *disciples who will last* is that it is God's strategy to grow his church!**

5. It's God's plan to win the world!

What is the one command that Jesus has left for us to achieve here on planet earth?

> **Matthew 28:18-19** *"Then Jesus came to them and said, 'All authority in heaven and on earth has been given to me. Therefore **go and make disciples of all nations** …' "*

To make disciples. Where? **In all nations!** God's plan for his church has the **whole world** in mind. God doesn't just want a little bit here, and a little bit there! He has a vision to bring the **whole world** to be disciples of his Son, Jesus.

And the reason that God has placed Jesus as Lord over his entire creation?

> **Philippians 2:9-11** *"Therefore God exalted him to the highest place and gave him the name that is above every name, that at the name of Jesus every knee should bow, in heaven and on earth and under the earth, and every tongue confess that Jesus Christ is Lord, to the glory of God the Father."*

God wants **every knee** to bow before Jesus. He wants **every tongue** to confess that Jesus Christ is Lord. Ultimately we know this will be true. Everyone who has ever lived **will** one day bow their knee before Jesus – either reluctantly on the last day as they face the consequences of God's judgment – or joyfully – anytime they hear the message of Jesus and become a Christian.

God has a plan for this universe – and it's to bring all things to be subject to Jesus.

> ***Ephesians 1:9-10*** *"And he made known to us the mystery of his will according to his good pleasure, which he purposed in Christ, to be put into effect when the times will have reached their fulfilment — **to bring all things in heaven and on earth together under one head, even Christ**."*

Okay – we get the picture. But here's the big question: *What **method** has God put in place to make disciples of all nations?*

Sometimes I like to think that God's method should be to fill enough stadiums in the world with huge audiences where great preachers will bring in the kingdom of God one stadium at a time! **But you know that's not the plan!** Jesus equipped his first followers with the power of the Holy Spirit so that **they** might be the messengers who took the gospel to the nations of this world!

> ***Acts 1:8*** *"But you will receive power when the Holy Spirit comes on you; and you will be my witnesses in Jerusalem, and in all Judea and Samaria, and to the ends of the earth."*

We continue that apostolic pattern! We get to reach out to others with the message of Jesus, grow them as faithful disciples, and then equip them to **go and make more disciples**... who will make more disciples... who will in turn make more disciples! The kingdom of God does not grow one stadium at a time; the kingdom of God grows **one life at a time**.

When we invest time and effort into a believer to help them be a faithful disciple, and instil in them a vision that they will go out and make yet more disciples, who will make even more disciples – then we are helping to achieve the mission that Jesus has set before us – that we will make *disciples of all nations.*

This book is all about how to turn new believers into lasting disciples. I have been a full-time local-church youth pastor for over thirty years. My experience is with young people. The stories I will tell all come from the strange world of youth ministry. The methods we have used have all been targeted at young people. **But the biblical principles will apply to any age group.** So whoever you are ministering to – whatever age group you work with – whatever situation you find yourself in – my prayer is that together we will discover effective ways of taking new believers on a path of discipleship that will end up changing the world for Jesus!

Can you think of anything that would be more satisfying and rewarding than that?

6. Before we go on – a warning!

When it comes to following up new believers, I suspect that the Christian church often falls into one of two errors:

a) *Not being faithful with new believers and "allowing" them to slip through the cracks.*

b) *Thinking that if we can come up with the world's perfect follow-up programme, then* **no-one** *will ever slip through the cracks!*

A lot of this book will be directed towards "Attitude (a)" – that is, practical ways to make sure that we don't lose new believers by neglect. But just before we move on, can I alert you to the danger of "Attitude (b)". You need to know this up front – **there is no sure-fire follow-up programme that guarantees no-one will ever walk away!** It is not within our power to ensure that every new believer stays on track. That is God's domain. We need to be faithful in everything we do – but ultimately it is God who causes people to grow.

As Paul explains to the Corinthians:

> **1 Corinthians 3:6** *"I planted the seed, Apollos watered it, but God made it grow."*

One of the things that has kept me sane through the decades of disciple-making among young people is the parable that Jesus told about the man who sowed seed in four different types of soil. Do you remember it? *(You can look up the entire parable – and its meaning – in Mark 4 v 2-20)* The four different soils produce four different results. But here's the thing to keep in mind: **a plant starts to grow in three of the four scenarios – but in only one survives to the end.** The seed that was planted in the rocky soil – it sprang up quickly, but did not survive because its roots were shallow. The seed that was planted in the thorny soil certainly grows – along with the weeds that eventually choke and kill it. To the sower it would have initially looked as if he was having a 75% success rate (3 out of the 4 start growing), but in the end he would have to conclude that he only had a 25% success rate (only the seed in the good soil keeps growing and produces fruit).

I don't think Jesus told this story to give us a mathematical formula for following-up new believers. But I think part of the power of this parable is to encourage us when, despite our best efforts, new believers do fall away and do not continue their journey to become world-changing disciples.

One of the sad things about working with young people over many years is seeing kids who **look** like they are responding to the message of Jesus – where you see some **initial** growth – but who do not last through to the end and who never start producing fruit. There is nothing that can describe the heart-break when this happens, and many of you will have experienced this first hand. The parable of the sower at least prepares us for the possibility that it might happen. But if any new believers do fall away, I want to be assured that it wasn't because **we didn't do our job**. I want to know that we made **every effort we could** to keep them growing. If a new believer does fall away despite our best efforts, then with reluctance we accept that they themselves chose not to continue.

But is discipling others **really** the best way to achieve effective ministry? Let's check out what Jesus did!

Chapter 2

The discipling method of Jesus

1. How Jesus spent his time [1]

I want you to imagine in your mind a picture of Jesus. A picture of Jesus "doing ministry". Any picture at all. What came to your mind?

I love the scenes where Jesus is doing the big, spectacular stuff. I love to picture him walking on water, stopping the storm, feeding the 5000, healing the sick or raising the dead! Or maybe preaching to the multitudes – from the mountain or from a boat. Or perhaps when he locks horns with the religious leaders. My picture of Jesus is always big and spectacular.

And he certainly did demonstrate the amazing power of God to thousands of people. But if you analyse how he spent most of his time over his three years of ministry, **that's not what he mainly did**. He invested most of his time into twelve very ordinary blokes.

He called them to himself and devoted the best part of the next three years to their lives. He walked with them, taught them, ate with them, settled down for the night with them, laughed with them, cried with them, corrected them, encouraged them, questioned them, trained them

---

1. I briefly looked at some of this material in *Fruit That Will Last* – to help leaders understand a biblical strategy for youth ministry. But I want to check it out in more detail here as it is **fundamental** to understanding Jesus' method of discipling

and commissioned them for ministry. He put up with their misunderstandings, their inadequacies, their failings, their brashness, their judgmental attitudes and their selfish desires. He took twelve very ordinary men and transformed them into a discipleship team that not only changed the then-known world, but who now continue to be a major influence across the planet some twenty one centuries later.

Extraordinary! Jesus was the Son of God! Presumably he could have summoned any power he liked from his heavenly Father to achieve his earthly mission. He could have organised big events for tens of thousands of people where he could have taught them and transformed them. He could have called down fire from heaven to show the righteousness of God. He could have put together the most awesome worship music that would have softened the heart of the hardest unbeliever. If he wanted to, he could have enlisted a heavenly choir to be his backing singers and unleashed the powers of nature to convince people to follow him quick smart.

And yet he invested his life into twelve ordinary blokes (and one of them was Judas!). If you had asked Jesus at some stage during his ministry how many people he had enlisted for his kingdom, and he had answered *"Twelve"* – would you have been impressed? And remember – he didn't enlist twelve world leaders; he didn't sign up twelve millionaires; he didn't take the twelve leading businessmen of Israel and create with them a corporate plan which would delight the shareholders; he didn't recruit twelve rock stars or media celebrities who would instantly command a following from a gushing public. He took under his wing a motley collection of doctors, fishermen, tax-collectors and political wannabees who were so transformed by him that they went on to change this world throughout every generation.

If you ask the question: *Why did Jesus spend his time this way?* – the answer lies in what the aim of his mission was. He didn't spend his three-year ministry racing around trying to win the whole world single-handedly. He didn't set up ministry programmes that attracted the crowds and dazzled them with his style. That's because his aim was not to have a spectacular three-year ministry and then see the whole thing collapse when he left! *(And I know that none of you would do that either!)* His aim was to make disciples of all nations. His aim was that because of his three years of ministry, every person in every land – in every era – would hear about his saving work on the cross and be challenged to respond.

If you then ask a second question *"Was his strategy of discipling twelve men successful?"* – the answer lies in the person reading this book! *(Yes, you!)* I don't know who you are, or where you live, or where you're at in your journey of faith. So let me tell you about *me* – you can substitute your own name and your own details – and you can work out whether Jesus' aim of *making disciples of all nations* was actually accomplished successfully through his strategy of discipling twelve men.

> As I sit writing this book, I am living in Australia. This is a country *never even envisaged* at the time Jesus told his followers to make disciples of all nations. I am writing this book in the early years of the twenty-first century – a time period *never imagined* in the years Jesus ministered on planet earth. And yet in this obscure nation at the wrong end of the world, living nearly two thousand years after the death of Jesus, I myself am a disciple of Jesus – and I am

surrounded by thousands and thousands of others who have chosen to become disciples as well.

I am assuming your situation is not vastly different from mine. But here is my point: the fact that there are now two billion disciples from every nation, tribe, language and tongue around this planet – some twenty-one centuries after Jesus completed his three year discipling ministry – proves that his method was successful! So if you're planning to have an impact for God's kingdom; if you're planning to significantly grow your church; if you're aiming to establish a relevant and life-transforming youth ministry – **why would you use any other method?**

And yet my bookshelves are full of books and resources on youth ministry that advocate *every other method imaginable!* If only you can run the right youth programme. If only you can run a great games night. If only you can get the kids on a camp. If only you can build an awesome worship band. If only you can invite guest performers and Christian celebrities to tell their story. If only you can have wiz-bang preachers. If only you can get your theology right. If only you can have community service programmes. If only you can do enough fund-raising. If only you can run a really "big event". If only you can have a dynamic website. There is a never-ending array of ideas and techniques to help people build significant youth ministries – and while there might be nothing *wrong* with any of the ideas they suggest – **wouldn't it be crazy to try and build a ministry and ignore the method that Jesus used?**

Jesus' aim wasn't to build a spectacular ministry programme. His aim was to make disciples of all nations. And his chief method for achieving this was to invest his life into a small number of people over a sustained period of time so they could be equipped to go and make more disciples… who would then make yet more disciples. And more. And more. One life at a time.

Can we have a quick peek into Jesus' ministry – and check out how **he** discipled other people?

2. Jesus' discipling strategy

Right near the beginning of Jesus' ministry – just as he is choosing his twelve apostles – we get a summary statement of his entire discipleship strategy:

> **Mark 3:13-15** *"Jesus went up on a mountainside and called to him those he wanted, and they came to him. He appointed twelve — designating them apostles — that they might be with him and that he might send them out to preach and to have authority to drive out demons."*

When we read Luke's account of the same incident, we get an insight as to what Jesus was doing on the mountainside:

> **Luke 6:12-13** *"One of those days Jesus went out to a mountainside to pray, and spent the night praying to God. When morning came, he called his disciples to him and chose twelve of them, whom he also designated apostles."*

Jesus spent the night in prayer – because there was a very important decision he needed to make: *Who would he disciple for the next three years?* This was no small matter for Jesus. This was his central strategy to *make disciples of all nations.* Jesus knew he needed to spend the night in prayer over such a key issue *(you would do the same, wouldn't you?).*

Let's look at his key strategy for transforming new believers into world-changing disciples:

a) He brought them in

> **Mark 3:14** *"He appointed twelve — designating them apostles..."*

Jesus' first strategy for making disciples is to call them to himself. He takes people and challenges them to completely change the direction of their life by submitting to him as Lord.

b) He built them up

> **Mark 3:14** *"He appointed twelve — designating them apostles — **that they might be with him...**"*

Once Jesus has called on believers to follow him, he invests into their lives. Those six words *"that they might be with him"* describe what he would do for the next three years. This is his master plan – to invest into their lives in such a way that they will be transformed from head to toe, and then equipped to teach more and more disciples in just the same way.

Which leads to step three:

c) He sent them out

> **Mark 3:14** *"He appointed twelve – designating them apostles – that they might be with him **and that he might send them out to preach...**"*

There is a purpose, a result, an outcome that Jesus is after by investing the next three years into these men. He wants to equip them so that they will know how to go and make more disciples in the same way that Jesus had discipled them. This is Jesus' central strategy to reach the world – and that same strategy has been handed down to us in the twenty-first century so that we might reach the almost seven billion inhabitants of planet earth.

The discipleship strategy that I want to outline in this book is one which the master discipler himself used. Programmes will come and go; cultural trends will come and go; but the main method that Jesus used to expand the kingdom of God was to invest sustained time and effort into a handful of believers.

And when you read the rest of the Gospels, you see Jesus using this method time and time again.

3. The master discipler in action

Let's pick a sample of how Jesus invested into the lives of his twelve disciples. Come with me on a fast skating trip through Luke chapters 8 and 9.

a) He involves them as he ministers

> **Luke 8:1** *"After this, Jesus travelled about from one town and village to another, proclaiming the good news of the kingdom of God. The Twelve were with him…"*

As Jesus moves about the countryside proclaiming God's kingdom, he takes the Twelve with him. Why do you think he did this?

b) He explains his teaching to them

He then tells the parable of the sower. When he finishes, the disciples come and see him privately because they're not sure what he meant. And it's to them, and them alone, that he gives the explanation of the parable.

> **Luke 8:9** *"His disciples asked him what this parable meant."*

I wonder why Jesus taught this way?

c) He teaches them about their new relationship

> **Luke 8:19** *"Now Jesus' mother and brothers came to see him, but they were not able to get near him because of the crowd. Someone told him, 'Your mother and brothers are standing outside, wanting to see you.' He replied, 'My mother and brothers are those who hear God's word and put it into practice'."*

If you were one of Jesus' disciples, and you heard him describing you as someone who was like his *mother or brother* – what effect would it have on you?

d) He involves them in his miracles

Jesus and his disciples are out in a boat. A storm whips up and threatens to destroy them. Have a look carefully at what Jesus is doing – and what his disciples' role is:

> **Luke 8:24** *"The disciples went and woke him, saying, 'Master, Master, we're going to drown!' He got up and rebuked the wind and the raging waters; the storm subsided, and all was calm."*

I sometimes wonder – why was Jesus asleep at this desperate point of need? Why did the disciples need to wake him? Jesus could have done the whole thing without their involvement. What was he teaching them by allowing things to pan out this way?

A little further on the journey, Jesus is surrounded by a crowd. There is a woman in the crowd who has been bleeding for twelve years. Here's what happened:

> **Luke 8:44-45** *"She came up behind [Jesus] and touched the edge of his cloak, and immediately her bleeding stopped. 'Who touched me?' Jesus asked. When they all denied it, Peter said, 'Master, the people are crowding and pressing against you'."*

Interesting. Why does Jesus respond by asking who touched him? Perhaps he wants to draw out the faith of this woman, but it's interesting that the first person to speak up is Peter, one of his Twelve. Jesus could have done the whole miracle without Peter's help, but for some reason, he allows him to get involved.

When they get to Jairus' house (his daughter has died), look carefully at how Jesus proceeds as he brings her back to life:

> **Luke 8:51** *"When [Jesus] arrived at the house of Jairus, he did not let anyone go in with him except Peter, John and James, and the child's father and mother."*

You can understand why Jesus lets the girl's father and mother come in. But why does he take Peter, John and James? He doesn't **need** them there. So what's he trying to show them? What's he trying to teach them?

e) He sends them out to minister

> **Luke 9:1-2** *"When Jesus had called the Twelve together, he gave them power and authority to drive out all demons and to cure diseases, and he sent them out to preach the kingdom of God and to heal the sick."*

Jesus now sent the twelve out to do **exactly what he himself had been doing** – casting out demons, healing sickness, and preaching the kingdom of God. *How did they know what to do? When did Jesus train them?* Does this answer our questions as to why Jesus was involving them in every stage of his ministry?

f) He cares for them after they've ministered

After their first attempt at ministry by themselves, look at what Jesus does:

> **Luke 9:10** *"When the apostles returned, they reported to Jesus what they had done. Then he took them with him and they withdrew by themselves to a town called Bethsaida…"*

The disciples tell Jesus all about what happened when they went out and ministered in his name, and then he takes them aside to spend some time with them. We don't know what they did during this time, but I wonder if Jesus was caring for them after they'd given of themselves so much in ministry?

g) He involves them in his miracles – again

Their time alone is short-lived because a large crowd follows them. The disciples notice there is no food for anyone, and they come to Jesus with a suggestion that the crowd be dispersed so they can all buy food. Look carefully at how Jesus replies to their suggestion:

> **Luke 9:12-13a** *"Late in the afternoon the Twelve came to [Jesus] and said, 'Send the crowd away so they can go to the surrounding villages and countryside and find food and lodging, because we are in a remote*

place here.' **He replied, 'You give them something to eat'.***"*

Why did Jesus reply this way? Why didn't he simply say *"Okay fellas – watch carefully – I'm gonna feed all 5000 in one hit!"*? He seems to be inviting his disciples into the decision-making process. They mumble out a reply of sorts:

Luke 9:13b-14a *"They answered, 'We have only five loaves of bread and two fish – unless we go and buy food for all this crowd.' (About five thousand men were there.)"*

Jesus wants to involve them further:

Luke 9:14b-15 *"But he said to his disciples, 'Have them sit down in groups of about fifty each.' The disciples did so, and everybody sat down."*

Now, you and I know how this story finishes. We know that all 5000 men (and all the women and all the children) are going to be fed – fully satisfied – with lots of leftovers. *But what method does Jesus use to turn five loaves and two fish into food for a multitude?* Watch carefully:

Luke 9:16 *"Taking the five loaves and the two fish and looking up to heaven, he gave thanks and broke them. Then he gave them to the disciples to set before the people. They all ate and were satisfied, and the disciples picked up twelve basketfuls of broken pieces that were left over."*

Jesus could have used any method he liked to multiply the loaves and fish. *But he chose to involve his disciples.* Now, here's a question for you. *What did Jesus give to his disciples?* Did he give them enough food for 5000 (that is,

Jesus had already miraculously multiplied the food), *or did he simply give them five loaves and two fish* (that is, the miracle happened in the hands of the disciples)? The text here simply states that after Jesus gave thanks for the five loaves and the two fish, he gave **them** to the disciples. I think the verse means: *"He gave five loaves and two fish to his disciples"*. When Mark reports this same incident, he seems to support this view:

> **Mark 6:41** *"Taking the five loaves and the two fish and looking up to heaven, he gave thanks and broke the loaves. Then he gave them to his disciples to set before the people.* **He also divided the two fish among them all.***"*

Whatever the fine detail, can you see that Jesus purposefully and deliberately involves his disciples in this miraculous event? Jesus' mission isn't just to feed hungry people; and his purpose isn't simply to bring glory to God; *but by the very method Jesus employs, he is teaching a discipleship lesson to his Twelve!*

h) He involves them in his prayer-life

The very next verse in Luke following the feeding of the 5000 says something very remarkable:

> **Luke 9:18** *"Once when Jesus was praying in private and his disciples were with him…"*

Did you get that? Praying in private **and** his disciples were with him. Why did Jesus do that? If he wanted to pray in private, he didn't need his disciples there! What's he trying to teach them?

i) He challenges their faith

Jesus asks his disciples what people are saying about him *(Luke 9:18-19)*. But then he turns the blowtorch on the disciples themselves:

> **Luke 9:20** *"'But what about you?' he asked. 'Who do you say I am?'"*

Whatever else Jesus was doing with his disciples, he wanted to challenge them so that they could clarify exactly what their faith meant to them.

j) He expands their understanding

Jesus then goes up onto a mountain, where Moses and Elijah appear, God the Father speaks from heaven, and Jesus is transfigured. That is – he is seen in all his resurrection glory. But notice who Jesus takes with him:

> **Luke 9:28** *"About eight days after Jesus said this, he took Peter, John and James with him and went up onto a mountain to pray."*

He takes three of his disciples along to witness what happens on that mountain. Why did he do this? What effect do you think it would have had on them?

k) He corrects their errors

There is a man whose son is seized by an evil spirit. This man had come to Jesus' disciples and asked for their help.

> **Luke 9:40** *"I begged your disciples to drive it out, but they could not."*

Whatever the disciples did, they were not able to minister effectively to that situation. Jesus deals with it in *Luke 9:42.*

Both Matthew and Mark then record a private conversation that occurs between Jesus and his disciples after this event:

> **Mark 9:28-29** *"After Jesus had gone indoors, his disciples asked him privately, 'Why couldn't we drive it out?' He replied, 'This kind can come out only by prayer'."*

Jesus dealt with all the mistakes and the misunderstandings that his disciples had. If you read through the rest of Luke 9, you will see him help his disciples understand a variety of issues.

I) He gets them to train others for ministry

> **Luke 10:1** *"After this the Lord appointed seventy-two others and sent them two by two ahead of him to every town and place where he was about to go."*

The Bible gives us no clue as to the role of the Twelve as this expanded group of seventy two are sent out to minister to others. But I have often thought: *"I wonder how these seventy two believers knew what to do in ministry?"* I wonder – could it be – that each of the twelve took six others, and trained them, and went with them? This is guesswork on my part – but it certainly fits a pattern.

- In *Luke 8,* Jesus is ministering with the Twelve watching.

- In *Luke 9,* Jesus sends out the Twelve on their own ministry trip.

- In *Luke 10,* does each of the Twelve now take six others and train them the same way that Jesus had just trained them?

Whether this model of discipling occurred on this particular occasion I do not know. But it does fit a pattern that we see throughout the scriptures. In Jesus' mission to *make disciples of all nations,* he brings followers to himself, he builds them up by investing his life into them, he then sends them out *to go and reproduce that transformation in the life of someone else!*

We have skimmed through a mere two chapters in the ministry of Jesus. Why don't you check out the full eighty nine chapters of the Gospels, and see if you can discover this same recurring discipleship pattern? That is, when Jesus brings his disciples to follow him, he then intentionally invests into their lives so that they will be equipped to go and do the same with others.

Does this sound like a discipleship model that's worth imitating? Well, let's check out how *Paul* went about continuing his mission to expand the kingdom of God *one life at a time!*

Next chapter!

Chapter 3

The discipling method of Paul

1. Paul's ministry with Timothy

Many, many people came to faith through the apostle Paul. He stood up for Jesus at a time when it was politically unwise to do so. He took the message of Jesus to the Gentile world – which upset the Jewish Christians back in Jerusalem. He preached defiantly to people who responded by trying to run him out of town. He planted and pioneered churches in umpteen places. He witnessed for Christ even while being held captive in a Roman prison. He strengthened those early believers by writing messages of encouragement, and who knows how many millions of people across all ages have come to follow Jesus by reading those very same letters preserved for us in the New Testament!

I can get so carried away by the gung-ho nature of Paul's ministry that I often forget about his personal discipling ministry, that was at the very centre of how he advanced God's kingdom. As an insight into how Paul discipled, can we check out his pastoral relationship with a young church leader named Timothy?

We're not quite sure how Paul and Timothy met, but it looks possible that Timothy was a convert from Paul's first missionary journey. Certainly, Paul invited Timothy to accompany him on many of his subsequent ministry trips, and Timothy was Paul's "right-hand man" on many occasions. We don't have a lot of details about the day-today interaction between Paul and Timothy as they spent extended time together taking the message of Jesus to places near and far. But when Paul writes to Timothy later in his life, we get a glimpse into what must have been an intensive discipling relationship.

I want to look at just one chapter of what Paul wrote to Timothy – from *2 Timothy chapter 1* (and I'll sneak in two verses from the beginning of chapter 2!). Let's discover the closeness of their pastoral relationship, as well as the intentional strategy that Paul had to transform Timothy from a new believer into a world-changing disciple.

2. Paul's discipling relationship with Timothy
from 2 Timothy 1

a) It was a deeply personal relationship

- *2 Timothy 1:2, 4* "To Timothy, my dear son … Recalling your tears, I long to see you, so that I may be filled with joy."

Paul did not just have a "professional" relationship with Timothy. He wasn't just a "senior pastor" to a "junior pastor". He treated him like a son, and used fatherly wisdom to point him in the right direction time and time again. *(See also 1 Timothy 1:2, 1:18 and 2 Timothy 2:1)*. I suspect any discipling relationship will include an element of this close relationship. You don't disciple someone because your name's on the rota – you develop a relationship with them that is close and personal. You love them as Jesus would.

b) He constantly prayed for him

> *2 Timothy 1:3* *"as night and day I constantly remember you in my prayers."*

I am very challenged by this one. I have been privileged to disciple numbers of believers over the years, but I'm not sure I can honestly say I have constantly prayed for them. If you want to transform a new believer into a world-changing disciple, then your passion for them will be reflected in your constant prayers.

c) He encouraged his faith

> *2 Timothy 1:5* *"I have been reminded of your sincere faith, which first lived in your grandmother Lois and in your mother Eunice and, I am persuaded, now lives in you also."*

He assures Timothy that he sees a genuine faith growing in him. This can be so important if you are discipling a new believer. The more recently someone has become a Christian, generally the less certain they will be about their faith. When I was cleaning out my bookcase one day, I came across a number of pamphlets I had bought in my first year or two of being a Christian. Nearly every one of them was entitled something like: *"How do I know my faith is genuine?"* or *"Am I really a Christian?"* Paul takes every opportunity to encourage the faith that he sees developing in Timothy. If God gives you the privilege of training someone else as a disciple, then it's important you keep strengthening their faith as well.

d) He activated his ministry gifts

> *2 Timothy 1:6* *"For this reason I remind you to fan into*

flame the gift of God, which is in you through the laying on of my hands."

God's Holy Spirit gives ministry gifts to every believer. But sometimes these gifts can sit under-developed, or even unused. One of the key roles of training a disciple is to help them to "plug in and turn up the volume" on any ministry gifts that God has planted in them. There is no doubt that Timothy had been gifted by God – there is plenty of evidence of those who had been strengthened through his work. Paul longs to see Timothy unleashed in ministry! Indeed it is the very purpose of him writing these two letters. *(Read through both 1 Timothy and 2 Timothy in full to see Paul's passion for Timothy's ministry.)*

e) He urged him to stand up for Jesus

2 Timothy 1:7-8 "For God did not give us a spirit of timidity, but a spirit of power, of love and of self-discipline. So do not be ashamed to testify about our Lord, or ashamed of me his prisoner. But join with me in suffering for the gospel, by the power of God…"

How would you feel if the person who had been the most influential in your development as a Christian was now chained in a dungeon because of their faith in Jesus? All sorts of fears must have been racing through Timothy's mind as he thought about the predicament that Paul was in. So many things can sidetrack a growing believer. Paul's desire for Timothy was that he would stand strongly for Jesus **no matter what!** That is the sort of brave faith we want to develop in anyone whom we are strengthening as a disciple.

f) He taught him God's word soundly

2 Timothy 1:13 *"What you heard from me, keep as the pattern of sound teaching…"*

How did Timothy know how to understand the scriptures? How did Timothy know what to teach to his young congregation? He was trusting that Paul had taught him God's word soundly. He would no doubt repeat to others the teachings that Paul had sown into him. That's how you grow disciples! You teach them God's word in such a way that they will be able to instruct and train others. Paul himself was the model so that Timothy knew how to do this.

Listen to the encouragements Paul gives to Timothy:

2 Timothy 2:15 *"present yourself … [as] a workman … who correctly handles the word of truth."*

2 Timothy 4:2 *"Preach the Word…"*

Paul knows that Timothy is able to follow these exhortations because **Paul himself has faithfully taught God's word to Timothy already!** This also needs to be true of anyone who is looking to transform a new believer into a world-changing disciple. In everything you do, keep teaching them God's word so that both of you keep living a life that is worthy of Jesus.

g) He warned him not to wander away

2 Timothy 1:14 *"Guard the good deposit that was entrusted to you – guard it with the help of the Holy Spirit who lives in us."*

Paul knows the danger of taking for granted what has been taught to you as a Christian. Timothy has had stacks of stuff "deposited" into him while growing as a believer. He has the gospel of Jesus planted in his life; he has the word of God growing in his life; he has a faith which keeps him trusting Christ, and no doubt Paul has "deposited" much into Timothy's life as he has trained him as a disciple.

Paul warns Timothy in his first letter:

> **1 Timothy 6:20-21** *"Timothy, guard what has been entrusted to your care. Turn away from godless chatter and the opposing ideas of what is falsely called knowledge, which some have professed and in so doing have wandered from the faith."*

If you are growing a younger Christian in their faith and pointing them towards maturity, then they need to know the danger of taking the things of God for granted. They need to be warned about false teachings and wrong doctrines that will lead them away from Jesus. They need to know the peril of no longer depending on the power of the Holy Spirit and trying to do it all by themselves.

h) He urged him to stand in God's grace

> **2 Timothy 2:1** *"You then, my son, be strong in the grace that is in Christ Jesus."*

It's easy to forget about God's grace. It's easy to think that somehow it's all up to us. The truth of the scriptures is this: that anything we do is only a response to God's grace. It is his unfailing love that keeps us going – it is not our unfailing faith! Being a strong disciple for Jesus is not something that we can achieve for ourselves. It is only God's love – it is only God's grace that causes any of us to keep standing strong.

I have seen "discipleship programmes" that simply keep

demanding a higher and higher standard from the disciple. Almost as if the amount of hard work we put in will determine our status in heaven! And I have seen young believers "burnt out" by having to achieve such unrelenting and unforgiving standards. Being a world-changing disciple is not about working harder and harder for God, hoping that one day he will approve of us. He **already** approves of us because of what Jesus has done for us in his death and resurrection! That's what Paul means when he says *"be strong in the grace that is in Christ Jesus".*

3. Paul's strategy for discipling

If you don't read any further in this book, but simply sow into another believer the eight things that Paul sowed into Timothy (as outlined above), then you will probably have a fruitful and vital discipling relationship which will honour God as you extend his kingdom.

But if you stay with me for a moment longer, we have just arrived at the absolutely key verse in the Bible that shows how the strategy of discipling one life at a time can build and multiply God's kingdom here on earth. Take a deep breath – here is the **key verse** in the whole Bible to set you on a biblical discipleship strategy for life:

> **2 Timothy 2:2** *"And the things you have heard me say in the presence of many witnesses entrust to reliable men who will also be qualified to teach others."*

This strategy spells out what Jesus himself started. This method continues the proclamation of God's kingdom in a way that causes it to multiply. This is the best approach ever to grow your church or your youth ministry. This is God's master-plan to bring the whole world to Christ.

Ready? See if you can grab the *generational flow* of this discipleship strategy. Here we go!

Step 1 – *"And the things you have heard me say"*

Paul invests his life and teaching into Timothy.

Step 2 – *"in the presence of many witnesses"*

Paul is not just sowing into Timothy's life, but into *many witnesses* as well. This is where the multiplication strategy of discipling all starts.

Step 3 – *"entrust to reliable men"*

What are Timothy and all the other witnesses meant to do with what has been deposited into their life? *Pass it on to other reliable people!* Are you now seeing how the whole discipleship strategy is ready to explode? How many *reliable people* can these *many witnesses* invest into? Dozens more than Paul could do by himself!

Step 4 – *"who will also be qualified to teach others"*

The *reliable people* are to be equipped and qualified so that each one of them can also disciple and teach others.

Here is the key to this biblical discipleship plan: you don't just equip and train a believer to make them a faithful disciple; you equip and train them in such a way **that they will be able to teach and disciple others**... who can teach and disciple others... who can teach and disciple others...

Here's what I want to emphasise: taking a new believer and transforming them into a world-changing disciple isn't just a "one-off" ministry that you do to help an individual believer. It's a **whole strategy** for building the church and expanding God's kingdom. And how do I know it works? It's a strategy that Jesus himself used – and then we see it continued throughout the rest of the New Testament.

This is not a strategy that will give you *instant results.* If you want to double the numbers at your youth group inside four weeks, this is not the way to go. There are no hi-tech programmes or wiz-bang activities. There are no overnight successes. But anything worth achieving takes time to grow. Whether it is training to be an astronaut, or winning a gold medal, or raising a child to be a responsible adult – there are no "quick fix" short cuts. Years of solid work are required to produce a great outcome. It is no different when it comes to producing lasting disciples who will grow God's kingdom and change the world for him.

But if you're prepared to build for the long-term, if you want growth that doesn't just have numbers but has a solid basis, if you truly want to see the world changed for Jesus, then start small, build strong. There are nations of this world who are depending on our faithfulness in growing the disciples whom God has placed into our care. And here's the surprise – when we start small by building the disciples around us, **it doesn't stay small for long!** As each generation multiplies its effect by training more and more believers in this systematic way, you will end up with a vast number of disciples **far more numerous** than any "instant programme" could ever produce!

So – how do I effectively transform someone from a new believer into a world -changing disciple? How do I get the whole process started?

Read on!

SECTION 2

Getting Disciples Started

Chapter 4
Why the gospel matters

1. The right foundation

If you want anything that you build to last, you have to make sure you start with the right foundation. Whatever you build something on will influence it right through to the end. If your foundation is solid and lasting, it will support what you build all the way through. But if your foundation is shaky, or insecure, or vague, or weak, then whatever you build will have a tendency to collapse.

This is the principle behind Jesus' *Parable of the Sower (Mark 4:2-20)*. The end result for each of the plants **depends on the quality of the soil it was planted in**. This is the principle behind Jesus' story of *The Two House-builders (Matthew 7:24-27)*. The end result for each of the houses **depends on the quality of the foundation it was built on**.

So, if you're going to build a world-changing disciple, what is the foundation that you want to build them on?

There is no doubt in the Bible what the essential foundation is to grow a disciple. It is **the gospel**. Nothing could be clearer!

> **Romans 1:16** *"I am not ashamed of the gospel, because it is the power of God for the salvation of everyone who believes."*

The gospel is the power of God to save those who believe. The power doesn't come from our presentation, or our persuasive words, or our clever marketing; the power to change people's lives comes from the gospel.

> **1 Corinthians 15:1-2a** *"Now, brothers, I want to remind you of the gospel I preached to you, which you received and on which you have taken your stand. By this gospel you are saved."*

We'll get to this verse in more detail a little later, but for the moment, can you note two things about the gospel from this verse?

a) A disciple must take their stand on the gospel.

b) The gospel will save you.

If the Bible is clear on how important *the gospel* is to build a new believer, then we need to check *what **the gospel** really is!*

2. The right news

The word that is translated *gospel* in most modern versions of the New Testament comes from the original Greek word – *eueaggelion* – literally *good news.* It is the announcement of something fantastic – it is the proclamation of a victory. When something magnificent has happened, you race around and tell anyone who will listen. That's the *good news.* That's the *gospel.*

So what's this good news all about? To find out, I checked through every use of the word *eueaggelion* in the New Testament. You will discover that every time the Bible uses the phrase *"the gospel of…"* or *"the good news of…"* there are only six words or phrases used to describe what this *gospel* or *good news* is all about.

a) It's the gospel of God

Eight times in the New Testament, the gospel is called *the gospel of God.[1]* The good news is a message from God, and it is a message about God. It's not a message that we have made up – and it's not a message that we have the freedom to change. If we're going to build world-changing disciples, we need to make sure their foundation is in *the gospel of God.*

b) It's the gospel of Jesus

How does God let us know his message about himself? Through his Son Jesus! Eleven times in the New Testament, the gospel is called the *gospel of Jesus,* or *the gospel of Christ,* or *the gospel of [God's] son.[2]* So whatever message we are proclaiming to turn someone's life around, we'd better make sure that message is about Jesus. The message that we use to bring a person to Christ and to build them as a disciple isn't primarily a message about them achieving their destiny, or reaching their potential, or accomplishing satisfaction and fulfilment, or, indeed, "giving their heart to God". If we want to be confident that it is *the gospel* that people are responding to, then we need to make sure that our message is primarily about Jesus. I guess that's why the four records about Jesus in the New Testament are called *Gospels.*

c) It's the gospel of the kingdom

Three times Matthew describes the gospel as *the gospel of*

---

1. Mark 1:14; Romans 1:1, 15:16; 2 Corinthians 11:7; 1 Thessalonians 2:8-9; 1 Timothy 1:11; 1 Peter 4:17.

2. Romans 1:9, 15:19; 1 Corinthians 9:12; 2 Corinthians 2:12, 4:4, 9:13, 10:14; Galatians 1:7; Philippians 1:27; 1 Thessalonians 3:2; 2 Thessalonians 1:8.

the kingdom.[3]   That is, this powerful message is not just about an individual's response, or a change of heart, but the message that Jesus proclaimed was that there was a brand new kingdom being established. Jesus himself was the king sent by God – and he announced by word and action that this kingdom was now being established for all those who would join. Building a new believer into a world-changing disciple is never just about helping an individual to mature in Christ; it is about establishing and extending the kingdom of God. Jesus called followers to his kingdom that they might be instrumental in growing his kingdom. Growing disciples need to understand that they are kingdom workers with kingdom values. This is the message that Jesus proclaimed!

d) It's the gospel of salvation

The great news of God's kingdom is that we can be saved from our sins. No longer does our rebellion against God lock us out of his kingdom forever. There is new life available through the mighty victory that Jesus has won. This is how Paul describes *the gospel* to the Christians in Ephesus:

> **Ephesians 1:13** *"And you also were included in Christ when you heard the word of truth, the **gospel of your salvation**. Having believed, you were marked in him with a seal, the promised Holy Spirit."*

Do you see how powerful this gospel is?

- *It is the gospel of salvation.*
- *It is the word of truth.*
- *It includes you in Christ.*
- *It marks you with the Holy Spirit.*

---

3. Matthew 4:23, 9:35, 24:14.

So if we want to build lasting disciples, we need to take the time to make sure we get the gospel right. There is a lot at stake!

e) It's the gospel of God's grace

Once again, Paul describes the gospel to the Christians at Ephesus this way:

> **Acts 20:24** *"However, I consider my life worth nothing to me, if only I may finish the race and complete the task the Lord Jesus has given me – the task of testifying to the **gospel of God's grace.**"*

This message that we proclaim is all about *God's grace.* The best definition of *grace* that I ever heard was *"when you do something for someone that they don't deserve".* If this life-changing message is *the gospel of God's grace,* it is a declaration that God has done something for us that we do not deserve. In the person of Christ, God has forgiven our sins, made us his children, bestowed on us eternal life, taken our punishment and saved us from hell. Whatever *the gospel* is, it is always a message about **what God has done for us, not what we can do for God**.

f) It's the gospel of peace

Paul's third description of the gospel to the Ephesians is this:

> **Ephesians 6:14-15** *"Stand firm then, with the belt of truth buckled around your waist, with the breastplate of righteousness in place, and with your feet fitted with the readiness that comes from the **gospel of peace.**"*

This verse is part of a passage that describes the Christian's armour – the Christian's battle-uniform. Verse 15 shows that one of the key elements in standing up to the attacks of the devil is for Christians to be focused on the *gospel of peace*. When Jesus achieves his mighty victory over Satan, and smashes every one of Satan's weapons, the result is peace. Peace between God and us. Peace among every element of God's creation. Peace for eternity. This is a very powerful gospel!

3. The right message

I have heard all sorts of messages used to help people say "yes" to Jesus. All sorts of stories, all sorts of emphases, all sorts of challenges. Some of these were one-on-one conversations; some of these were public messages preached from a stage. The key question when anyone makes a first-time commitment to Jesus is this: *Is what they just heard* **the gospel***?* That is, did they hear the message that God says has the power to save them? Were they challenged to build their life on a solid foundation that will never let them down? Or did they merely hear a *cheap substitute* for the gospel?

In a church I once visited, they had an international guest speaker who preached a message at their youth group. He was a godly man; he brought a powerful message; and a number of students responded. Here is a summary of his message:

- *Moses was a man who lived his life with strengths and weaknesses.*
- *One day he met his moment of truth when he encountered God.*
- *That moment of truth changed his life.*

> • *Have you come to your moment of truth? Will you give your life to God tonight?*

A number of students responded. People were very impressed. His message was from the Bible. His challenge was powerful. But here is the key question: *Did he proclaim the gospel?* And if he *didn't* proclaim the gospel, **what did the students respond to**?

Biblically, I think this is the key issue: **if the gospel has not been proclaimed, and people respond, can we say that they have responded to the gospel?**

So let's check it out: **what does God say are the essential elements of *the gospel?***

Next chapter!

Chapter 5

Get the gospel right!

So – what does the Bible say *the gospel* is? If you wanted to explain it to someone else, what would you need to talk about? And if you want to give a growing disciple the best foundation ever – indeed, the only foundation that will see them through – **what is this key message that has the power to save those who believe?**

Let's check out what two of Jesus' apostles understood by *the gospel*. Rather than looking at individual messages preached in the New Testament, I have chosen two key passages where the Bible writers **tell us** what they mean by *the gospel*.

1. Paul's understanding of the gospel

When Paul writes to the Corinthians, he explains the gospel to them at the beginning of Chapter 15 [1]. Let's check out what he says:

a) The gospel will save you

> *1 Corinthians 15:1-2 "Now, brothers, I want to remind you of the gospel I preached to you, which you received and on which you have taken your stand. By this gospel you are saved, if you hold firmly to the word I preached*

---

1. Paul also introduces his letter to the Romans with some key points about the gospel. See Romans 1: 1-6.

to you. Otherwise, you have believed in vain."

There has to be a response to God's gospel. It is the announcement of great news. But it must be acted on. It must be received. It's the solid rock that you must hold firmly to. Jesus' victory over sin **is** what saves us. On the cross, Jesus took our sin, our punishment, our guilt and our hell. If we want to see people saved, they must make their response to the gospel. Because that's what saves us! [2]

b) It's about Jesus' death

> *1 Corinthians 15:3-4a "For what I received I passed on to you as of first importance: that Christ died for our sins according to the Scriptures, that he was buried..."*

Okay – now we're getting down to the business of *"what is the gospel?"*! Paul states clearly: *"For what I received I passed on to you as of first importance"*. So – what are the key elements of the gospel that are of first importance? Here's the first one: *"That Christ died for our sins according to the Scriptures"*. Jesus' death on the cross is absolutely central to the gospel. It **is** the gospel! The reference to Jesus being buried emphasises this. What the burial shows us is – **Jesus really died!**

c) It's about Jesus' resurrection

> *1 Corinthians 15:4b-5a "that he was raised on the third day according to the Scriptures, and that he appeared..."*

The declaration of Jesus' victory is also about his

---

2. See also Mark 1:15, Acts 15:7, Romans 1:16-17, Galatians 3:8, Ephesians 1:13, 3:6, 2 Thessalonians 2:14, Colossians 1: 5-6.

resurrection.[3] This is the second key element of the gospel. It's not just his death. Jesus' death without his resurrection makes no sense. They are simply the two halves of the one saving activity.

The references in 1 Corinthians 15 to Jesus' appearances after his death emphasise the actuality of his resurrection. Paul was writing to people who **had actually seen Jesus after he had risen**, as he highlights in verse 6:

> ***1 Corinthians 15:6*** *"After that, he appeared to more than five hundred of the brothers at the same time, most of whom are still living…"*

2. Peter's understanding of the gospel

In Acts chapter 10, Peter explains the very centre of God's plan. He details what the key message really is.

Let's listen in:

a) It's about Jesus being Lord

> ***Acts 10:36, 38*** *"You know the message God sent to the people of Israel, telling the good news of peace through Jesus Christ, who is Lord of all … God anointed Jesus of Nazareth with the Holy Spirit and power, and how he went around doing good and healing all who were under the power of the devil, because God was with him."*

However we explain the gospel, it is always a message about Jesus. A message that declares that Jesus is Lord.

---

3. See also 2 Timothy 2:8.

b) It's about Jesus' death

> ***Acts 10:39*** *"We are witnesses of everything he did in the country of the Jews and in Jerusalem. They killed him by hanging him on a tree."*

And we'll see the effects of this death in just a moment…

c) It's about Jesus' resurrection

> ***Acts 10:40*** *"but God raised him from the dead on the third day and caused him to be seen. He was not seen by all the people, but by witnesses whom God had already chosen — by us who ate and drank with him after he rose from the dead."*

Once again – the proof that Jesus was physically raised from the dead was the vast array of witnesses who saw it for themselves.

d) It's about Jesus coming as judge

> ***Acts 10:42*** *"He commanded us to preach to the people and to testify that he is the one whom God appointed as judge of the living and the dead."*

This is an integral part of the gospel which it is easy for us to overlook. It probably doesn't fit our twenty-first century notion that "everything is tolerated, and there really are no absolutes".

But God takes our sin very seriously, and one day will deal decisively with those who have refused to turn to him. The appointment by God of Jesus as judge of the living and the dead is seen by the Bible as being central to the gospel.[4] [5]

e) It's about forgiveness

Acts 10:43 *"All the prophets testify about him that everyone who believes in him receives forgiveness of sins through his name."*

That's why Jesus' death really matters. He died so that we will be forgiven. Everyone who believes receives forgiveness of sins through his name. What a marvellous and gracious gift the gospel is!

That's what Peter believed was central to the gospel. That same gospel should be our basis for bringing a new believer to faith.

3. Getting our understanding right

As I look through the scriptures, there seem to be different ways of sharing the truth of the gospel. Different things get emphasised to a variety of listeners from diverse cultures and backgrounds. There is no rigid formula which must be repeated word perfect every time.

The gospel is not just a matter of getting our words right and listing every bullet point in order. When we declare the lordship of Jesus in the victory of his death and resurrection, we enter a spiritual arena where we are totally dependent on God to work a miracle. That's what making disciples is all about.

But it seems to me that, however you explain the gospel,

---

4. See also Romans 2:16; 2 Thessalonians 1:8; 1 Peter 4:17; Revelation 14:6-7.
5. While Paul's message at the Areopagus (Acts 17:16-18) might be seen at *pre-evangelism,* the theme of judgment is still evident (Acts 17:31).

your message must contain these *unchangeable biblical essentials:*

- Jesus is Lord, and calls on you to submit to his lordship.

- Jesus has died for you so that you can be forgiven.

- Jesus has risen for you so that you can have eternal life.

There are strong warnings in the Bible about proclaiming a different message – presenting a different gospel – or pointing people to a different saviour.

> **2 Corinthians 11:3-4** *"But I am afraid that just as Eve was deceived by the serpent's cunning, your minds may somehow be led astray from your sincere and pure devotion to Christ. For if someone comes to you and preaches a Jesus other than the Jesus we preached, or if you receive a different spirit from the one you received, or a different gospel from the one you accepted, you put up with it easily enough."*

Paul's main point to the Christians in Galatia is that they had fallen for a different gospel.

> **Galatians 1:6-11** *"you ... are turning to a different gospel — which is really no gospel at all. ... If anybody is preaching to you a gospel other than what you accepted, let him be eternally condemned! ... I want you to know, brothers, that the gospel I preached is not something that man made up."*

We need to check if the gospel that we are presenting is the same gospel that the Bible presents. The centuries might have changed; the culture might have changed; the communication methods might have changed – the language might have changed; but the gospel from God – which has the power to save those who believe – **will never change**.

Some of you are now wondering why I am spending so much time on *getting the gospel right*. Surely it is clear from the scriptures that the gospel is a message about Jesus' death and resurrection. What's all the hassle?

Here's my observation: many of us have a problem *really believing this*. There is a strong temptation to present a slightly softer message – a slightly more palatable message – a message that it might be easier for an enquiring person to say *"yes"* to.

I find this to be a temptation when I am sharing the gospel in a one-on-one situation. I find this to be a temptation when I am sharing the gospel by preaching to thousands.

> I received a phone call once from a very well-known youth evangelist. His organisation had been presenting a number of large youth rallies around my city, where students were being called on to give their life to Jesus. He wanted to take me out to lunch. And then he said to me *"I want to find out why you're not bringing your students to my rallies."* (Gulp!)
>
> I was somewhat in awe of this man. He had been mightily used by God to transform the hearts of thousands of teenagers. He was acknowledged as one of the best youth communicators in the world. I was feeling slightly nervous as he asked me that key question: *"Why don't you bring your students to my rallies?"*
>
> I found my reply hard to get out, but eventually, these words stumbled from my lips. *"The main*

problem is your preaching. You say in your brochures that you proclaim the gospel. But here's the message I heard you speak at your last rally."

I then proceeded to give him a summary of what I had heard him proclaim in a previous message. *"Nothing in this world makes sense. Only Jesus does. No-one else has any answers. Jesus does. No-one else can fix your problems. Jesus can. Come forward and give your life to Jesus."*

He agreed that that was a fair summary of his message. And hundred of young people had responded!

But my comment to him was: *"If the gospel is about the death and resurrection of Jesus, and the forgiveness that comes through his name, then there was nothing in your message that was remotely connected to the gospel."* That was the essential reason why we were not bringing our students.

"But I want the maximum number of students to respond!" he protested. He was genuinely worried that if he focused on the death of Jesus, he would not connect as well with his audience, and he might not achieve the results he had been getting.

I challenged him to proclaim a cross-centred message and trust God to look after the response. And to his credit – at his next rally – he did! And a huge number of students responded!

I find that many people are tempted to hold back from the gospel because they're scared it won't work. But if we want to produce lasting disciples, we need to make sure that they start their journey well. We need to check that they have the right foundation. That's why the *way* we call them to Christ really matters. We need to get the gospel right!

And if we can get the *content* of the gospel right, how do we make sure that our message is *clear?*

Read on!

Chapter 6

Make your message clear

Step 1. Make the gospel clear

So – why go to all this trouble to work out what *the gospel* is? Simple. If our aim is to help a new believer be transformed into a world-changing disciple, then we need to get the *foundation* right. That is, the rest of this believer's life will be built on the gospel. **If we make the gospel clear, then we have a much better chance of producing a lasting disciple!**

So it's worth taking the time and effort to help ensure that the *way* we bring a new believer to faith is the best way possible. It matters!

> Some time ago I received a phone call from a colleague of mine who headed up a large inter-denominational youth ministry. They were instrumental in running huge youth events that attracted thousands of teenagers. Indeed, that coming Saturday, we were taking a few busloads of our kids to a large city-wide rally that she and her organisation were conducting.
>
> She rang me because she wanted to video some high-schoolers telling their story of how they came to faith in Jesus. She wanted to use some of these video clips in the rally that Saturday. She asked me: *"Do you have some students who could tell their story of coming to faith in Jesus, whom we could video the next day after school?"*

I was honoured to be asked and assured her that I could make some students available. But then I asked her: *"The church you attend has a very large youth ministry. Why haven't you videoed some of the students from your own church?"*

I could hear the faint tone of distress in her answer. *"We've already videoed a number of our own students, but we can't use any of them. Our students were excited; our students were passionate; but not one of them could explain what Jesus had done for them in forgiving them and calling them into God's kingdom."*

She wanted to call new believers into a lifetime of active service for Jesus. So she took the time to get the gospel right. If you start people on the wrong road, you'll never get them to their correct destination. If you give people a message that is not the gospel, then you make it hard to bring them to be lasting disciples.

If you're in charge of running an event which has an "up-front" gospel proclamation, then you can ensure that the message the speaker gives is indeed true to the biblical gospel. But at other times you will have no control over that. Your students might be at an event which is organised by another ministry group completely. So how do you ensure that your young people hear an accurate gospel message?

Simple really! **You make sure that the gospel is shared with them in the beginning stages of their follow-up!**

This is our first key for growing lasting disciples. If someone has just made a commitment to Jesus, we must ensure that we go through the gospel again with them at the first available opportunity. Who knows what they have already heard? Who knows which bits they really understand? Even with the best gospel presentation possible, it's entirely possible that the young person you are now following-up was only half-listening!

So take the time to walk them through the gospel again. We usually do this by taking students through the *Discovering Jesus* Course.[1]

The five basic steps in this course are:

  i. **Discovering God** (*includes the information that God cannot stand our sin*)

 ii. **Discovering me** (*includes the information that all of us are sinful and deserve God's punishment*)

iii. **Discovering Jesus** (*about who He is*)

iv. **Discovering Jesus' death** (*we see how this is God's way of dealing with our sin*)

 v. **Discovering my response**

If a person who responds only has a vague idea that *"they've given their heart to God"* – while they may well have made a true commitment to Jesus, they need more clarification if they're going to continue on as a faithful disciple. We do them a disservice if we do not explain the gospel clearly to them.

So, Step One in growing a lasting disciple: get their foundation right – *make the gospel clear*!

---

1 This 5-week course, which is aimed at 11-14s, takes a new believer through the basic steps of the gospel to help them know what they are committing themselves to. *Discovering Jesus* is available through The Good Book Company.

Step 2. Make the cost of discipleship clear

What does it cost a person to become a Christian? Answer – nothing! Jesus has paid the complete cost himself. (This is the great news of the gospel!). But what does it cost a person to **keep on** being a Christian? Answer – everything! When you follow Jesus you need to surrender everything to him – including your life. If you want to be a faithful disciple of Jesus, **it will cost you everything!**

If you want to produce lasting disciples, **they need to understand this cost before they start the journey!**

This is the principle that Jesus teaches in *Luke 14:*

> **Luke 14:28-30** *"Suppose one of you wants to build a tower. Will he not first sit down and estimate the cost to see if he has enough money to complete it? For if he lays the foundation and is not able to finish it, everyone who sees it will ridicule him, saying, 'This fellow began to build and was not able to finish'."*

And again in the next verse:

> **Luke 14:31-33** *"Or suppose a king is about to go to war against another king. Will he not first sit down and consider whether he is able with ten thousand men to oppose the one coming against him with twenty thousand? If he is not able, he will send a delegation while the other is still a long way off and will ask for terms of peace. In the same way, any of you who does not give up everything he has cannot be my disciple.*

One of my concerns is that we sometimes encourage new believers to start their journey of faith **without first weighing the cost!** No wonder that they tend to stumble along the way! How many people do you know who have started the journey with Jesus – but not continued? Do they fit the description that Jesus gave in *Luke 14:30* – *"This fellow began to build and was not able to finish."*?

How do we help disciples to finish strong? **By letting them know the cost before they start the journey.** Look at the way that Jesus calls people to follow him in Matthew's Gospel:

a) Discipleship involves repentance

Here is Jesus' call for people to follow him:

> *Matthew 4:17* *"From that time on Jesus began to preach, 'Repent, for the kingdom of heaven is near'."*

Following Jesus involves repentance. That is, you must turn **away** from doing things that **dishonour** Jesus, and turn **to** doing things that **honour** Jesus. Your life must change! If a person becomes a follower of Jesus without realising this, they are in for a rude shock – and they probably won't last long!

I met a young man down at the shopping mall. His friends, who already came to our youth group, introduced him to me. He appeared to be kind of spaced-out on drugs.

"You're that Christian bloke, aren't you?" he exclaimed. *"I'm a Christian too. I became a Christian last week."*

"That's fantastic" I replied. *"Tell me how you became a Christian!"*

"Dunno. Happened at that church down the road. They had a great band – they asked people to come forward – I went out the front with all the other people and some guy prayed for all of us."

"Great!" I said. *"What else happened?"*

"Nuffin. After this guy prayed for all of us, they sent us back to our seats."

"Since then?" I enquired.

"Nuffin."

"So…" I mumbled, starting to be a little sceptical by this point. *"What's different about your life now that you've become a Christian?"*

"Nuffin much!"

Do you get the feeling that this young man is on a very short journey as a "Christian"? Not only did he have very little concept of *the gospel,* but it appeared he had no idea of *repentance!*

If you want to produce lasting disciples, then it pays to ask a *repentance* question very early in your follow-up – preferably at the same time that they are becoming a Christian.

You could ask a couple of questions like:

> *"If you commit your life to Jesus, what are some of the things that you're currently doing that you know you'll need to stop?"*

> *"If you commit your life to Jesus, what are some of the things that you're currently **not** doing that you know you'll need to start?"*

b) Discipleship involves sacrifice

This emphasis on repentance is clarified by the **context people were in** when Jesus called them to follow him.

> **Matthew 4:21-22** *"Going on from there, he saw two other brothers, James son of Zebedee and his brother John. They were in a boat with their father Zebedee, preparing their nets. Jesus called them, and immediately they left the boat and their father and followed him."*

When James and John said "yes" to Jesus, they left their fishing boats behind. Now think about this. They were fishermen. They earned their money by catching fish. By leaving their fishing gear behind them, they were giving up their income to follow Jesus!

A little later on, Jesus calls Matthew (Levi) to follow him.

> **Matthew 9:9** *"As Jesus went on from there, he saw a man named Matthew sitting at the tax collector's booth. 'Follow me,' he told him, and Matthew got up and followed him."*

Matthew was a tax-collector. He earned a commission on every tax he collected. For him to leave his tax booth behind meant giving up his only means of income. Luke makes this point even more plainly:

> **Luke 5:28** *"and Levi got up, **left everything** and followed him."*

If you want to produce lasting and fruitful disciples, then they need to know from the word "go" that they need to be prepared to give up **anything** to follow Jesus.[2]

Ivan[3] was a tough Year 9 boy at a tough boy's high

---

2. See also Matthew 8: 19-22, and Matthew 19:16-26, where Jesus goes out of his way to help potential believers understand the sacrifice that they will need to make.

3. I told this story in more detail in *Fruit That Will Last* – Chapter 3. I think it is worth repeating here!

school. He used to sit in my scripture class, and was often the source of trouble. He was captain of the school soccer team, and his goal in life was to become a professional sportsman. He appeared to have very little interest in Christian things.

One week, on a scripture worksheet that gave him the opportunity to give a personal response, he wrote down that he wanted to become a Christian. Quite frankly I didn't think he understood what that meant. I caught up with him at lunchtime.

"So what's this about you wanting to become a Christian?" I enquired.

"That's right. I want to follow Jesus."

So we met after school one afternoon so we could talk. As we chatted, I still kept getting the impression that he did not understand what he was doing. I did not think he had any concept of treating Jesus as his Lord, or of submitting to him.

I was searching for what to say. He told me he had a girlfriend. So I pushed him on this.

"What if I told you that to start following Jesus you had to give up your girlfriend and never see her again?"

I wanted to challenge him on whether he was prepared to put Jesus No. 1. His answer was unexpected.

"O sure – no worries – I'll give her the flick straight away!"

Hmmm. Teenage boys! They still don't know how to treat a lady. Wrong question. And then I hit on it! The perfect question.

"What if I were to tell you that to become a Christian, you had to give up playing your sport, and never play it again?"

"Hmm ... that's a hard one"

We talked for the next half hour or so. We talked about the cost of being a committed follower of Jesus – we talked about the implications of having your whole life changed around by Christ.

Eventually, Ivan said

"If I've got to give up rugby to follow Jesus, I'm prepared to do it."

I knew he was ready. I led him to Christ, and sent him off to be the best athlete he could possibly be!

c) Discipleship involves ministry

Sometimes people become followers of Jesus believing that they can get all the benefits without having to take any of the responsibility. If you look at the way Jesus calls his followers, he cuts off this misunderstanding right at the start.

Matthew 4:19 *"Come, follow me," Jesus said, "and I will make you fishers of men."* [4]

Right up front, Jesus shows his new believers that when they make the choice to follow him, they also make the choice to be on his ministry team. There is work to be done; there are fields ripe for harvest; and Jesus is signing up a

---

4. We will refer to getting new believers into active ministry many times in this book. Not only because this step is so crucial, but also because it is so often *left out!* More details of this step are provided in Chapter 18.

workforce who will join with him in the world-wide task to make disciples of all nations.

You know the problem you sometimes have in churches of *getting Christians into ministry?* You can see so many things that can be done for the kingdom if only you could find enough volunteers willing to help! By spelling out the ministry requirement of any believer *right up front,* you can minimise the problem of breeding "lazy" Christians. Indeed one of the keys for keeping growing disciples *passionate* is to keep them in front-line ministries. (More about this later!) But the time to introduce them to a lifetime of disciple-making ministry is *right up front when they first make a commitment to Jesus.*

d) Discipleship changes every relationship

In fact Jesus emphasises the cost of placing him number one in your life so much, that he raises questions about the most protected and cherished relationships that we have – those within our own family. Listen in as he spells out the cost:

> **Matthew 10:34-37** *"Do not suppose that I have come to bring peace to the earth. I did not come to bring peace, but a sword. For I have come to turn 'a man against his father, a daughter against her mother, a daughter-in-law against her mother-in-law — a man's enemies will be the members of his own household.' Anyone who loves his father or mother more than me is not worthy of me; anyone who loves his son or daughter more than me is not worthy of me."*

This sort of teaching would not win Jesus the *Family Man of the Year Award* in the popular press! What he says is absolutely outrageous! But we know how much Jesus values family relationships – the Bible is full of exhortation to husbands, wives and children to urge them to be Christlike in all that they do. And yet – when you get on board with Jesus – **your relationship with Jesus overrides every other relationship that you have.** And while we need to be sensitive as to how we communicate this to new believers, they need to understand that their commitment to Jesus might cause disruption in their family when those near and dear to them do not understand. If we want to produce lasting disciples, we need to prepare them for this possible dislocation in their close relationships. If we do not forewarn them – we do them a disservice. And if we do not forewarn them – we set them up for failure.

e) Discipleship involves total surrender

Disciples need to understand from the outset that following Jesus means a total surrender of absolutely everything about their life. A total surrender of all possessions; a total surrender of all rights; a total surrender of life itself.

Jesus continues on in Matthew 10 – directly after the verses above:

> **Matthew 10:38-39** *"and anyone who does not take his cross and follow me is not worthy of me. Whoever finds his life will lose it, and whoever loses his life for my sake will find it."*

The parallel passage in Mark sheds some extra light on these verses:

> **Mark 8:34-37** *"Then he called the crowd to him along with his disciples and said: 'If anyone would come after*

me, he must deny himself and take up his cross and follow me. For whoever wants to save his life will lose it, but whoever loses his life for me and for the gospel will save it. What good is it for a man to gain the whole world, yet forfeit his soul? Or what can a man give in exchange for his soul?"

Jesus is making some very powerful statements as to what it means to be a disciple:

i. You must deny yourself

To follow Jesus, your own agenda drops to bottom place. You deny your right to have your own way. You deny that you are your own master. You have now totally surrendered to Jesus as your master.

ii. Take up your cross and follow him

To understand what it means to *take up your cross*, you need to work out: *"What did it mean for Jesus to take up his cross?"*

It meant he was prepared to face humiliation that he did not deserve. He faced suffering and death that he did not deserve. He was prepared to give up his life. He was prepared to surrender everything. To be a disciple of Jesus, you need to be prepared to give all this up too. It's only by *losing* your life this way that you will *save* it. If a disciple understands this at the outset, then they will be much better prepared for their journey

iii. Be prepared to give up the whole world

Imagine having possession of *the whole world*. Imagine you owned every amount of wealth the world had to offer; you had every power that generations of humans have dreamed about; you owned everything and everyone and you could do exactly what you wanted at anytime with anything. Jesus says: *"What good would that do you if you lost your relationship with God in exchange for that?"* Answer – Not one bit! Nothing is worth losing your life over!

If I offered you a deal – I would give you a million dollars and when you accepted it, I would shoot you dead – *that's a bad deal.* It doesn't matter how much you gain – if you lose your life over it, you will never enjoy it. If you gain everything the world has to offer, but lose your eternal life in the deal, Jesus says it's a bad trade. Don't take it!

Here's the sad thing. Most "disciples" who give up on Jesus, give up **for far less than the whole world**. They give up because there's a sin they want to hang on to. They give up because there's a relationship they want to hang on to. They give up because they're too busy, or too tired, or too bored.

New disciples need to understand that their commitment to follow Jesus is a commitment to **give up everything** – even their own life if that's what's needed.

If Step One in laying a solid foundation for a new disciple is to *make sure the gospel is clear,* then Step Two is to *make sure the cost of discipleship is clear.*

Step 3. Make the invitation clear [5]

The invitation to become a Christian – whether it is proclaimed in front of a crowd of thousands, or shared individually between two friends – needs to be clear. The potential believer needs to know exactly what they're saying "yes" to. If they're unsure of what they're responding to, it's unlikely that they'll stay on board for the whole journey.

We need to keep in mind the high likelihood that people may misunderstand some of our terms. So, if our invitation to a person is: *"Would you like to become a Christian?"* – while in one sense it is a perfectly clear question – because there are so many common misconceptions as to what it means to be a Christian, I suspect it is too vague to produce an accurate response.

While inviting people to share in the eternal life that Jesus has won for them in his mighty victory **should** be the easiest question in the world for us to ever ask of someone, for many of us (including me!) it can sometimes be the *hardest* question. But if we give an unclear invitation, then we will get an unclear response. And if a person starts their life as a believer with an unclear response, there's a high likelihood that they'll end up with a level of discipleship far less than what Jesus is expecting.

Here are the two common errors that I notice when it gets to actually asking the question and inviting people to follow Jesus:

---

5. The "altar call" is discussed in more detail in *Fruit That Will Last* – Chapter 17.

a) Our invitation is too vague

I hear preachers doing this all the time. They preach a great gospel message – then comes the time to ask for a response, and they issue an invitation *that's so vague*, that it is unlikely *anyone* knows what they're responding to!

Here's a few examples collected over the years (usually just before another invitation such as *"Come out the front …"):*

- *"If you want to give your heart to Jesus…"*
  (no other explanation)
- *"If you want to go to a new level in your relationship with Jesus…"*
- *"If you want to make a stand for Jesus…"*
- *"If you know this is your moment with God…"*

There's nothing essentially *wrong* with these invitations, but if our aim is to produce lasting disciples, these are *too vague* for the person who's interested to know what they're responding to.

I tried to work out why preachers sometimes give vague invitations. Deep down, I suspect it's because they do not trust the gospel. They're worried that if they give a very specific invitation, they might not get much of a response. So they water down the invitation to soften the blow and increase the potential responders.

Here's the difficulty: if you're wanting to produce lasting disciples, then you need to give them a clear idea as to what they're responding to. If we do not make this clear for them, we lessen the chance that their response is genuine.

b) Our invitation is too pushy

I have seen this happen – both in public evangelism and in one-to-one evangelism. The Christian is *pushing too hard* in trying to get a response. The potential believer is obviously not ready to make a commitment, but the "helpful" Christian is just pushing harder and harder trying to get them across the line.

Why do we sometimes do this? Once again, I suspect it's because we do not trust the gospel. We think it's up to us to keep pushing until we get a response. We're worried that if we gave a *less pushy* invitation, we might not get a response. But this sort of pushiness will never produce lasting disciples. If we want to make our discipleship work, then we need to make sure that our invitation for people to respond is clear.

c) A way forward

I understand the thinking of those who give both vague and pushy invitations. I think it goes something like this: *"If we can get as many people as possible to respond, it increases our chances of finding the **genuine responders** among them."* I understand this thinking, but I don't believe it works. I think it creates problems for those who are persuaded or cajoled into responding (but who are not making a real response). I have met many people who have been "burned" by this – and it makes it very hard to get a genuine response out of them on subsequent occasions. But I believe it also creates problems for those who are genuinely responding. If we want them to last the distance, they need to know what they are responding to.

Whenever I speak evangelistically, there are three specific

categories of people whom I will invite to respond:

i. Those who want to say "yes" to Jesus for the first time

For those who have heard what Jesus has done for them in his death and resurrection – and who realise that they have never made a commitment to follow him – I want to invite them to take this opportunity to sign up with Jesus for eternity.

ii. Those who have wandered away and want to come back

For those who have made a commitment of sorts some time ago, but have not stuck with it, and they know they've wandered away – and today is the day that they are coming back – I want to invite them to respond with the intention **that they will not wander away again.**

iii. Those who are not sure – and want to make sure

For those who are genuinely concerned whether they are indeed a Christian – and want to make sure – I want to invite them to come out and make sure.

I will then sometimes give a warning for two groups of people who I do **not** want to respond – this makes the invitation even clearer!

iv. Those who are just pretending

I want to make it clear that we're only looking for those who are genuine in their response. Those who are making a public commitment are asking everyone else to be witnesses that from this day onwards **they will be different**. I would ask people not to respond if they have no intention of changing their life for Jesus.

v. Those who are already keen Christians

Sometimes I need to tell the keen Christians that it's okay for them not to respond. The response time is for **those who are making a significant change**. So I often reassure our keen Christians: *"If you're powering on with Jesus, and you're plugged into your church, and you are faithful at attending your youth group and small group – you don't need to respond today. The response time is for those who want to make a significant spiritual step tonight."*

If our aim is to produce lasting disciples, then we need to be clear at the very beginning of the journey. The best way to help a disciple achieve a clear-cut result is to give them a clear-cut start. If you want to build a life that will last, it needs to be constructed on a rock solid foundation.

To help achieve the best possible outcome of growing disciples who will be passionate to change the world:

- Make the gospel clear, so they understand what it means to have Jesus as Lord.
- Make the cost of discipleship clear, so they know what they're committing to.
- Make the invitation clear, so they know what they're responding to.

So, if you can get your message to be *clear,* how do we best encourage someone's response to be *genuine?*

Next chapter!

Chapter 7

Encourage a genuine response

We've now established how important it is to start a disciple's journey on the right foundation. We need to make the gospel clear; we need to make the cost of discipleship clear; and we need to make the invitation clear.

The next key step is to make sure that our **initial conversation** with a new believer is one that will clarify their commitment. By making sure that they understand the life-journey that they have now commenced, we give them the best possible opportunity to keep on growing as a faithful disciple. This initial conversation is one of the keys to producing lasting disciples.

This initial conversation is most likely to take place at one of the following moments:

- If the new believer has responded at an organised evangelistic event, and there is time available for each new believer to catch up with someone on the response team, then this is a great opportunity for this initial conversation.

- If there is no time at the actual event, then this will be the first conversation you have with a new believer once your follow-up commences.

- If a person is coming to faith through a one-on-one situation, this conversation can happen at the same time they are making that commitment.

1. Double-check their decision

Encourage the new believer in the decision they are making, but don't automatically assume that they are ready to become a Christian. They might just want to ask some questions. There might be a personal issue they would like to work through. There's no use trying to disciple a person unless they're ready to start the journey!

2. Question their decision

Gently question and probe to help them clarify what they are really saying. This is better than just telling them lots of things.

> Ask: "Why would you like to become a Christian?"

> Ask: "What do you think a Christian really is?"

3. Fill in the gaps

From the answers to the above questions, start probing further to help them *fill in the gaps* where their understanding is inadequate. If the person gives an answer which shows that they really don't understand something, ask a question which will help them to see that they haven't quite grasped it yet.

> *The usual **first** answer to "What do you think a Christian really is?" is **"A Christian is someone who believes in God"**. (This answer describes almost everyone!) Question this by saying something like… "So if I just believe that God is there, does that makes me a Christian?" If the person says "yes", then you might say – "So it doesn't matter how I live at all – as long as I believe God exists?"*

*The usual **second** answer to "What do you think a Christian really is?" is **"A Christian is someone who obeys what God says"**. (This answer describes no-one!) Question this by saying something like... "So how often do you have to obey God – just when you feel like it, or all the time? And how many of his commandments do you have to keep? Just the ones you feel like – or all of them?" If the person replies by saying, "You need to obey all of God's commandments all the time", then gently ask, "How many people in the world do you think always do exactly as God says?"*

*The usual **third** answer to "What do you think a Christian really is?" is **"A Christian is someone who TRIES to obey God"**. You might ask, "So how hard do I have to try – just when I feel like it, or try as hard as I can all the time?" If the reply is "Try as hard as you can all the time", gently ask, "How many people in the world could honestly say that they've tried to obey God as hard as they can all the time?"*

By helping the person see that their answers are inadequate, you help them to search for a more correct understanding of what it means to follow Jesus. If you can get them starting the journey with a correct understanding, it will greatly help them to keep powering on as a faithful disciple.

Keep probing until either:

a) *The person is able to say clearly what makes someone a Christian, or...*

b) *The person realises that they don't really understand what makes someone into a Christian.*

4. Explain the gospel

This is a good opportunity to explain carefully what the great news about Jesus really means. It's not just a matter of believing in God, or even obeying him. The essence of understanding what it means to be a Christian is that Jesus has done it all by his death and resurrection, and all we have to say is *"yes"* as we submit to his lordship over our life.

There are many different ways to express this – and many other books that will give you lots of clues.[1] Just make sure that your explanation contains the biblical material outlined in the earlier chapters, and that everything points to Jesus' lordship as evidenced by his death and resurrection.

My favourite illustration of what it means to become a Christian is an adaptation of *The Record Book of Sin*, used in the superb training course published by *Evangelism Explosion*.[2] With their permission, I have included an outline of this gospel presentation in Appendix 5.

Make sure you use the Scriptures at this point. If you're working through a published gospel explanation, that will no doubt take you to the most appropriate verses. Here are some verses which might help you explain God's gracious offer of salvation:

> *John 3:16; Romans 10:9; Isaiah 53:6; 1 John 1:9; 1 John 5: 11-12*

---

1. An ideal leaflet is "Two Ways To Live – the choice we all face" published by Matthias Media.
2. *Evangelism Explosion* run training courses world-wide to help Christians in their personal evangelism. You can contact them at www.evangelismexplosion. org

5. Try and change their mind

This might seem like a weird step at this stage, but it will help the person clarify their commitment by challenging it; because at this point, a person will either be backing off: *"Maybe I'm not ready to become a Christian yet"* or getting keener: *"Yep! I want to become a Christian now"*. A good way forward is to try and talk them out of whichever position they are moving towards.

For the person who is saying "I'm not sure if I want to become a Christian now" – encourage them, and keep probing "What is stopping you from becoming a Christian?" "Do you see what you would miss out on if you say 'no' to Jesus now?"

For the person who wants to become a Christian, emphasise the cost of discipleship. "If you really became a Christian, what things would you need to change in your life?" (If they aren't sure of what should change, ask: "What things are you now doing that you might have to stop?" and "What things are you now NOT doing that you might have to start?" For this second question you can then go through the ideas of Bible reading, prayer, fellowship with other Christians, witnessing to their friends etc.)

If you think they might have wrong motives for becoming a Christian (e.g. their best friend has just become a Christian, or their parents are Christians, and they're just going along with it without really thinking about it), ask something like: *"What if I were to tell you that your best friend (or parent) has just given up on Christianity and reckons it was all a big mistake – would you still want to become a Christian?"*

6. Give them a choice they can say "yes" to

You need to be careful when you are talking with a person at a vulnerable point in their life. Particularly if they are younger than you. There can be all sorts of underlying pressure for the person to "make a commitment" for the wrong reasons. (e.g. *"I want my leader to like me"*).

So don't present them with a choice where they have to say *"yes"* or *"no"*. (*"So, are you ready to become a Christian now?"*). Sometimes it can be very hard for a person to say "no" in these circumstances.

Give them two choices where they can say *"yes"* to either one. (*"So, do you think that you're now ready to become a Christian, or would you like to think about it for a bit longer?"*) They can now give you an honest answer – without the pressure of having to say *"no"* to you. The more honest and thought-through their response, the more likely it is that they will become a lasting disciple.

7. If they're backing away...

If a person is backing away from making a commitment, there is no need to panic! It is not up to you to talk them into a commitment they are not ready for. God is in charge of this process, and he will bring their decision to fruition in his own time.

Here's a helpful way forward if the person is backing away from making a commitment:

a) Accept

It's important that the person knows that you have accepted their answer – whatever it is. If they are not ready to become a Christian, show them that you accept them, that you accept their answer and that you love them just the same.

b) Encourage

Encourage them that they are at least thinking about it, and encourage them to keep thinking about it. Perhaps give them some literature – maybe *Mark's Gospel* – and encourage them to come back to you and talk more. Keep the doors open. (This might be a good point to make sure you have some contact details to make it easier for any further follow-up.)

c) Warn

Throw in a note of warning. Make sure that they understand the consequence of their action. You might say: *"So, at the moment, you are saying 'no' to Jesus. So what would happen to you if you were to die in this state and stand before God to be judged?"* Communicate to them that you fully accept their answer – but make sure they understand the consequences of their answer.

8. Show them what they must do

Explain clearly what they will need to do now if they want to become a Christian. Basically, all they have to do is talk to God in prayer and ask him to make it happen.

Here's an easy way to help them to remember what to say to God in prayer. When they pray to God, they need to pray about **A, B** and **C**.

*A: **Admit** that I don't deserve God's help.*
(I am a sinner.)

B: Believe that Jesus died for me and rose to give me new life. *(Ask God's forgiveness for my sins.)*

C: Commit my life into God's hands. *(Ask Jesus to run my life his way.)*

Give them an idea of the sort of prayer that they will need to pray. *(A good example is in the back of "Two Ways to Live".)*

9. If need be, take the pressure off again

If you are at all worried that the person is going into something that they are not ready for – then give them one last opportunity to pull out with dignity. After you have explained clearly what they must do to become a Christian, you might say: *"Okay, what would you like to do? You can either become a Christian right now with me, or you can go home, think about it, and then tonight talk to God all by yourself. Which would you feel more comfortable with?"*

If they decide to go home and do it themselves, double-check that they know exactly what to do, and then ask them to get back to you in the next day or so to let you know how it went. Tell them: *"Even if you decide that you don't want to go ahead with it – please let me know, because I want to be able to help you."*

10. If they're ready, pray with them

If the person is really ready to become a Christian, and wants to do it with you right there, then suggest that you both pray. Ask them if they know what to say – assure them that their exact words don't matter because God knows what they really mean. Go through the **"A-B-C"** again, if necessary to reassure them.

A good idea is if you pray first – that God will help them and hear them, and then have the person pray the prayer of becoming a Christian when you have finished. Most people I have encountered have been able to pray out loud in this situation.

11. Get them to feedback what has really happened

When all this is done, try and get some feedback from them as to what they think just happened. This will further help you both to clarify how they're going. Ask questions like:

- *"How do you feel about what you've just done?"*

- *"Are you a Christian now?"* (And if they're unsure… *"Did you just ask God to make you a Christian? Did you mean it? So has he done it?"*)

- *"If you were to die right now, and God said to you 'Why should I let you into my heaven?', what would you say to him?"* (If they're unsure… ask: *"Did you just ask God to forgive all your sins?" "Did you mean it?" "So has he done it?" "So why should God let you into heaven?"*)

12. Arrange the next step

It is absolutely vital that this great conversation you have just experienced is linked in with what the *next step* is. So before your conversation finishes, try and ensure that the following steps have been taken:

- Introduce them to another Christian, so they get to explain their decision to someone else.

- Give them some literature that will help them take their first steps.[3]

- Give them a book of the Bible, so they can start exploring their new life. I prefer to give them Mark's Gospel, with a reading guide – and encourage them to find out for themselves everything they can about following Jesus. I believe an individual book of the Bible is more helpful at this stage, rather than a whole New Testament or a full Bible. Giving a new believer such a large book **might** just be overwhelming! (You can give them a full Bible a little later!)

- Arrange the next meeting. It is absolutely vital that this person meets again with you – or with another Christian – inside the next week. They are starting on an exciting journey – and these early steps are absolutely crucial.

- Assure them of your prayers.

- Write their details down so you can contact them – and give them your details so they can contact you. [4]

All this might sound a little complex and detailed. It's not meant to. All this is to help you be thorough and careful in how you lead a new believer to Christ. Remember, your aim isn't just to *get them to cross the line*. Your aim is to

---

3. There is a wide variety of literature suited to all different groups of people. The leaders at your church will be able to show you what they recommend.
4. There are more details on "Keeping Track" in Chapter 17.

transform a new believer into a world-changing disciple. This is a journey of many months and many years. By being careful in the way you bring them to Christ, you are helping them to be absolutely genuine in their ongoing walk with him.

And the first thing you will be preparing them for are the attacks of the devil.

Check out the next chapter!

Chapter 8

Understanding the Devil's weapons

When a person has made a decision to follow Jesus, what happens **immediately** really matters. And it's not just what you *do* that matters. What is of prime concern is that it is done **immediately**. The first few days for a new believer can be a mixture of pure exhilaration and pure terror.

Pure exhilaration because they're full of optimism; they're on a high; they have a new life; they have a new eternity; they're on a new mission; they're a changed person. But this can be mixed with pure terror. What have I got myself into? What if I fail? What if I don't last the distance? What if it's too hard? What if it's not real? The first 48 hours of a new believer's life can be **absolutely crucial** for their survival – because you can be certain the devil will use his two key weapons to try and reverse the spiritual decision that this person has just made. His two key weapons? Doubt and guilt.

Weapon #1 – Doubt

The devil's first attack is to cause a new believer to *doubt:* to doubt whether their decision is real to doubt whether they are genuinely saved; to doubt whether all this stuff about Jesus is actually true.

We can see the devil using this weapon against the first new believers. Here's the scene: God has created the first human beings – he has placed them in a garden paradise – he has provided everything for them – and he lives in unbroken fellowship with them. He has given one clear command:

> **Genesis 2:16-17** *"And the LORD God commanded the man, 'You are free to eat from any tree in the garden; but you must not eat from the tree of the knowledge of good and evil, for when you eat of it you will surely die'."*

The devil now moves in to cast doubt into the minds of the people God has created:

> **Genesis 3:1** *"Now the serpent was more crafty than any of the wild animals the LORD God had made. He said to the woman, 'Did God really say, 'You must not eat from any tree in the garden?'."*

*"Did God **really** say that? Surely that's not what he meant? You can't **seriously** believe that, can you?"* The devil's first weapon is to cause us to doubt. To question what's happened. To question God.

You can be assured this will be his first attack on any new believer. Within a few hours of a person making a decision to follow Jesus, the devil will be there with all guns blazing trying to introduce *doubt* into the equation. Why? **Because doubt is the opposite of faith! Faith** says, *"I trust you"*. **Doubt** says, *"I'm not sure if I trust you"*.

When Jesus called Peter to walk on the water – while Peter kept his faith in Jesus he was fine. But when he looked around at the wind and the waves, he started to doubt, and he started to sink. Jesus reached out to him to save him.

> **Matthew 14:31** *"Immediately Jesus reached out his hand and caught him. 'You of little faith,' he said, 'why did you doubt?'"*

On another occasion, when Jesus is teaching his disciples to pray with faith, he shows them how the opposite of faith is doubt:[1]

> **Matthew 21:21** *"I tell you the truth, if you have faith and do not doubt, not only can you do what was done to the fig tree, but also you can say to this mountain, 'Go, throw yourself into the sea,' and it will be done."*

Later on, Jesus reinforces this when he challenges Thomas to stop doubting, and believe:

> **John 20:27** *"Put your finger here; see my hands. Reach out your hand and put it into my side. Stop doubting and believe."*

The devil will try and convince the new believer to simply question and doubt the decision they have made. To either convince them that their *decision* is not real, or that *God himself* is not real. And if a person is in the first few days of their new life with Jesus, they are at the point where they are most vulnerable to giving up. That's why our ministry to them *in the first 48 hours* is so vital.

Weapon #2 – Guilt

The devil's next attack is to try and cause a new believer to *feel guilty* – to *feel like a failure* – to *feel condemned and crushed and worthless*. And to achieve this, the devil has a very simple strategy: he simply accuses us of our sins and lets guilt do the rest!

Satan's strategy is revealed in the last book of the Bible:

---

1. See also Mark 11:23. Jesus also challenges doubt in Matthew 28:17 and Luke 24:38, and James tackles it in James 1:6.

>*Revelation 12:10* *"For the accuser of our brothers, who accuses them before our God day and night, has been hurled down."*

You can almost imagine Satan standing before God accusing us – pointing out our every fault – pleading with God to condemn us and give up on us. And he accuses us directly too! Every believer knows how damaging Satan's accusations can be. And here's why his attacks hurt us so much: what he accuses us of *is basically true!* Yes, we have failed! Yes, we have sinned! Yes, we do deserve God's judgment! It is so easy to simply feel guilty, to feel like a failure and to quietly give up.

Guilt is such a heavy burden. No-one can stand it!

>*Psalm 38:4* *"My guilt has overwhelmed me like a burden too heavy to bear."*

No wonder the devil has a field day when he keeps reminding us of our sin! If we believe him, we will be easily crushed!

But that's why Jesus died on the cross! That's why we can know we have full and free forgiveness from God our father! That's why God does not give up on us, and why we have no need to give up on him! **But a new believer won't automatically think of this!** A new believer may simply feel they have failed God! A new believer may well be so weighed down by their own guilt that they will simply give up because they know they cannot live up to God's standard.

That's why our ministry in the first 48 hours really matters! This is extreme danger time for a new believer! That's also why getting alongside them *in the first week* matters so much!

Let's check out the crucial things that you can do in the first week of a believer's new life. *(Next chapter!)*

There are seven key ministries that I believe are absolutely critical in the first crucial week:

Hang on – just before we do that – can I clarify a term I am using? You will notice I keep referring to "follow-up" – that is, the ministry that we do with a person once they have decided to follow Jesus. I am using the term because I know that everyone understands what I mean. And I am happy enough to use it.

But there's something about the term "follow-up" that doesn't sit well with me. It almost suggests "what has already happened is the important bit – this is just an added-on extra". Like when you undergo major surgery – and a little later your doctor schedules a "follow-up" visit. We all know which meeting with the doctor was the important one – the one where you had major surgery! Your "follow-up appointment" is just to make sure everything's okay and that nothing has gone wrong.

I worry that this same thinking can translate into our disciple-making. That the presentation of the gospel where the new believer underwent spiritual surgery is the real deal, and this "follow-up" ministry is just a tacked-on extra. Just to make sure that it's still going okay, and that nothing's gone wrong.

Nothing could be further from the truth! *As*

*important as the initial evangelism is, the ministry that we have after that (the "follow-up ministry") is **absolutely crucial** to producing lasting disciples. Indeed, I believe that the missing ingredient in producing world-changing disciples is an under-valuing of this crucial follow-up ministry. This whole book is dedicated to making this "follow-up" ministry **the centre-piece** of building lasting disciples.*

So, now that I have all that off my chest, back to the seven key ministries that I believe are absolutely critical in the first crucial week!

1. Make a follow-up phone call immediately

Within the first 48 hours, you need to make contact with the new believer. A phone call to check how they're going. A phone call to head off their doubts. A phone call that shows them you care.

In this world of instant messaging, you can of course supplement your phone calls with SMS's, emails and blogs, but nothing replaces actual voice-to-voice contact.

Things that you would cover in this call include:

- *Ask them how they're going as a new Christian. Has it been wonderful? Has it been difficult?*
- *Assure them that you are continuing to pray for them.*
- *Check whether they've made a start with reading the bible for themselves. Encourage them along this path.*
- *Check whether they've experienced the devil's attacks of doubt or guilt. Warn them of this danger. Give them some Bible verses to help arm them against his attacks.*

- o *1 Peter 5:6-10*
- o *James 4:7-10*
- o *1 Corinthians 10:13*
- o *Ephesians 6:10-18*

• *Remind them of the step they've taken and the importance of perseverance.*

• *Pray* **with** *them. Yes – over the phone! It will greatly strengthen them.*

• **Plan the first personal contact.** *Don't finish your phone conversation until you have locked in a date that week for the two of you to catch up face-to-face.*

Special note when contacting children and teenagers: If the new believer is a child or a teenager (i.e. school-student age), then it's important that we include their parents in this follow-up. This is true whether their parents are Christians or non-Christians. You need wisdom to discern at what level you involve their parents – this might look very different for a 10-year-old compared with an 18-year-old!

Here are some tips to keep in mind:

• *Talk to the parents on your first phone call. This is a courtesy to them so they know who is contacting their child. With a younger child (e.g. primary school age), I would talk with the parents* **first** *and ask permission to speak with their child. With an older teenager, I might introduce myself to them after speaking with their child.*

• *Explain to the parents which church you are from, and the reason* **why** *you are contacting their child. With Christian parents whom you know well, it might well be appropriate to give them some details of their* *child's spiritual decision. With non-Christian parents whom you have never met before, it might be wiser to give them some more general information.* ("Your child has shown a real interest in the children's activities at our church, and I wanted to chat with them to see if I could invite them along next week. You, of course, would be most welcome to visit as well!")

- *Your own church will have procedures in place which deal with contact for those aged under 18. Make sure you fully comply with these.*

- *If a parent absolutely prohibits your contact with their child, then we must respect this. If God is genuinely calling their child to faith in such a hostile environment, then we must trust that he will bring that faith to fruition. Constant prayer will be our only weapon. Praise God – that prayer can't be prohibited! The best way to support a child in circumstances such as this is to see whether there are any Christian students their age who can get alongside them to support them at school or other activities.*

Colin was a teenage boy who got involved with our youth group. He was aged around 14, and his parents were quite hostile to Christian things. Strangely, they had sent him to a Christian school – because they weren't keen on the local state school, and they wanted their son to learn good "morals". His friends at the Christian school invited him to our youth group, and he made a genuine commitment to Jesus. His parents prohibited him from "being a Christian" at home (e.g. he wasn't allowed to read his Bible at home). Having a slightly rebellious nature, he would frequently disobey his parents by reading his Bible at home. They would punish him by sending him to his room. I asked him what he did when he was sent to his room, and he answered *"I read my bible"*. (Quite a disobedient boy, really!). God nurtured his faith – as an adult he married a Christian girl – and is now a full-time pastor in a local church!

2. Have your first face-to-face contact

It really matters to make a personal face-to-face contact *within the first week*. The phone calls are great, but nothing replaces actually caring enough to spend time with a person. This personal contact might be at the new believer's house, on your church property, or at a neutral venue. The location doesn't matter that much. But making it happen in the first week *really* matters.

Here are some tips to make this first face-to-face contact fruitful:

- *Follow up everything you said in your phone call.*
- *Take the opportunity to read the Bible with the new believer. If they're already doing this themselves, read along with them wherever they're up to. If they haven't started yet, then this is a great time to get them started. What you're doing here is modelling how to spend individual time with Jesus.*
- *Make sure you pray with them. Once again, use this as an opportunity to teach about prayer, and then model for them how to pray effectively.*
- *Be ready for lots of questions. It's okay if you don't know all the answers. But take a note of their questions, and let them know that you can get back to them with a more detailed answer.*

- **Plan the first event that this new believer will attend.** *We'll talk about this in a moment, but now is the time to get a firm commitment that you will bring them to a Christian event which will be their "next step" on their road to faith. Can you just notice the emphasis on "bring" them? Don't just invite them and hope they'll show up! Make an arrangement to pick them up, give them transport, arrive with them etc, so they don't have to face a new group "alone". Do not leave this first face-to-face meeting until you have a firm diary date for the next step!*

- *If you're working with someone under 18, your own church will have guidelines for how you can have face-to-face contact with them. Make sure you follow these guidelines so that the integrity of your ministry is protected.*

3. Take another believer along with you

This is a crucial step! *Take another Christian with you!* The ideal time to do this is at the first face-to-face contact. This other believer does not need to be a world expert in following up new Christians, but they are a vital part of the process of building lasting disciples.

Here's why this matters:

- *By taking another Christian with you, you start the process of widening the new believer's circle of Christian support.*

- *There is now one more person that they can turn to for help.*

- *If there are a number of people whom you need to follow-up, you can introduce this new believer to this person, who will become their primary carer when you move on to minister to other people.*

- *This extra person will bring their own perspective which will help the new believer have more well-rounded growth.*

- **This additional person should be the same age and gender as the new believer.** *You want a genuine friendship to develop. This becomes crucially important if you are following up someone who is in a different age-group from you. For example, if you are an adult, and you're following up a teenager, then take another teenager with you. Preferably someone from their own school or social network.*

- *The new believer gets to meet someone who is just like them. This will greatly encourage them!*

- *The "other Christian" gets to tell their story of how they came to Christ. This will encourage the new believer.*

- *The new believer gets to describe their journey of faith to somebody different.*

- *The new believer can now have twice as much follow-up. Not just you, but also the new person you have taken. This minimises the chances that the new believer will fall through the cracks.*

- **This is a crucial discipleship lesson for the new believer.** *They get to see that it is "normal" for an established believer to disciple a new believer.* **This will set their thinking in the right direction for *their* future ministry.**

- **This is a crucial discipleship lesson for the "other**

> **Christian"** *that you have taken along with you. This is where they will learn how to follow up a new believer. And how will they learn that? By watching you! (More about this later!)*
>
> • *And ideally, who should this "other Christian" be? Someone whom you are already discipling! Someone who was in the place of the new believer just a short time ago.*

4. Help the new believer with good resources

There might be some additional literature that you can take with you. Your own church probably has some suggestions of what you could use. I always find it handy for the new believer to have:

- *A Bible with a personal Bible-reading plan.*
- *A short pamphlet which outlines the step they took in saying "yes" to Jesus.*
- *A pamphlet or booklet which outlines the basic steps of Christian growth.*
- *A good Christian book to read*

You may have already given some of this out at the moment this person made their decision for Jesus. But now might be a good time to give them something additional. Don't overwhelm them with everything. And the way you resource a *keen reader* will be different from how you help a *reluctant reader*. But make sure they have *something* which will help them continue on in their journey.

Don't confine yourself to the print medium. Would they learn better from a DVD? Or the Bible on CD? Or a podcast? What about some helpful websites? Or online devotionals?

These media systems are in a constant state of change – so I am reluctant to list any, as they will probably have changed or gone by the time you read this! But ask the question – what would most help this new believer to grow *in a style where they will respond the most positively?*

> Craig was a boy in his mid-teens when he arrived at our church youth group. He didn't have much of a handle on Christian things, but seemed keen to keep coming. He made a genuine profession of faith, and we sought to keep growing him as a disciple. Despite our best efforts, he never really got into reading his Bible. And then we twigged as to *why.* He was a very poor reader! He had only just survived school. For him, reading was difficult and arduous. And here we were saying: *"If you want to grow as a Christian, you need to keep reading this 1000 page book!"* No wonder he was struggling!
>
> So we bought him the audio Bible on CD. He could explore the wonders of God's word without having to struggle with reading. A lasting disciple was now being made!

5. Bring the new believer to a Christian event

Again, notice the emphasis on *bring.*[1] Don't just invite them and hope they'll make it. Go out of your way, pick them up from their house, have a cuppa with them first, do whatever it takes so they don't have to arrive at your Christian event all alone.

---

1. I believe the distinction between *inviting* and *bringing* is an important one. See further details in Chapter 18.

Don't worry too much about *what* this Christian event is. It might be your special follow-up group for new believers, or it might not be. It could be a normal church service. Or your weekly youth group. Or your regular Bible study. It's not so crucial that you bring the new believer to the *perfect* event for them; what matters is that you bring them to *a* Christian event within the first week.

There are a number of reasons for this:

- It will introduce the new believer to the central place of Christian fellowship in their journey of faith. My experience has been that for most disciples, the one thing that has kept them going through tough times is their *fellowship* with other believers. It's important to instil this early into the thinking of a new believer so that they don't end up with an individualised faith that does not plug into the Christian community.

- It's important to introduce the new believer to *lots of other Christians*. Taking them to a Christian event is a great way to do it. If they are a teenager, it's particularly important to introduce them to lots of other teenagers at your church youth group.

- The new believer will learn heaps about the Christian life simply by observing other Christians. They will experience other believers praying, hearing God's word explained, praising God, giving generously, sharing personally etc – and by seeing them in action, they will learn the crucial steps that will help them in their own journey.

- It will be a huge encouragement to the Christians at your church to meet a new believer. They will be blessed because you brought your new person along.

• There will be stacks of other Christians who can now be part of the follow-up process. Once again, this minimises the risk that the new believer will *fall through the cracks.*

• As you drive home, it gives you and the new believer an opportunity to reflect on what just happened – to clarify what you learnt: and encourage each other in your faith.

6. Get the new believer started in ministry

When do you get a new believer started in ministry? *The moment they come to Jesus!* Being a disciple means being a disciple-maker.[2] The two are synonymous! You can't have one without the other!

Jesus calls people to follow him **and puts them on his ministry team straight away**. The call to follow Jesus is the call to become fishers of men. The best time to get new believers into active ministry is *straight away.* This doesn't have to be some fancy ministry that they sign up for. All they need to know is that now they belong to Jesus, he wants them to bring their friends to follow him as well. In fact, if you're moving nice and fast on this one, by the time you bring your new believer to their first Christian event, *they might already have **their** first new person with them!* [3]

Brad and Norman were two Year 10 students at the local high school. They had both made a

---

2. Matthew 4:18-20. For further details, check out Chapter 18.
3. I told this story in more detail in *Fruit That Will Last.* It bears repeating!

commitment to follow Jesus. The week after they became Christians, I caught up with them at school to plan the next step. I explained to them: *"You've got a whole lifetime of learning to follow Jesus ahead of you. We're going to help you every step of the way. Now the first thing I want you to know is that Jesus wants you to help your friends discover the things that you've just discovered".*

"You mean he wants us to help our friends become Christians?" asked Brad.

"Exactly!"

Brad and Norman looked at each other and smiled. They turned to me and said, *"We'll be back"*, and they disappeared into the schoolyard. A few moments later they returned with two friends in tow. *"This is Sam and Allen. They want to become Christians too!"*

New Christians are absolutely the best at bringing new people along to things. **New people bring new people.** I want them to have a passion for their unsaved friends from the word go. If they are new Christians, then they don't yet understand that the Christian Church is full of people who can't be bothered about having a ministry in this world. They will find this out later! But I want them to be passionate to minister to others right from the very beginning.

You are shaping habits and priorities which will be part of these young disciples' life for decades and decades. So start them off right – and prepare them for a lifetime of passionate and active ministry.

7. Plan your regular follow-up

The key ministry that you really want to start is this: that you will plug the new believer into their strategic ongoing follow-up ministry. Later on in this book, we will talk about exactly what this might look like. If you're working with adults, it might be a one-on-one mentoring programme.

Great caution needs to be exercised if doing one-on-one work with under 18s – for all sorts of legal and social reasons. Your own church will have guidelines for you. Usually it is better to work with under 18s in a small group.

The follow-up group you're planning might be the regular small bible-study group or home fellowship that you attend; or it might be a special group for new believers.

Whatever it is, it is crucial that within the first week you **plan this ongoing meeting**. Your new believer needs to understand that they need to be coached about how to live as a disciple. They need to know there is a whole new life to learn about. They need to know that we're going to walk with them every step of the way. They need to know that they are on a journey to become a world-changing disciple.

The follow-up group that you're planning might not start for a few weeks. But in the first seven days you need to have a plan in place so that the new believer knows that this is an ongoing ministry that they need to commit to.

Okay! You've survived the first seven days! What next?

Chapter 10

The best way to meet with disciples

1. You can't disciple in a large group

Here is my observation based on the last thirty years of discipling young people: *you can't do it in a large group.* Large groups have their place. They are an excellent way of developing a community. They are an efficient way of delivering information to a large number of people. **But a large group alone will never produce lasting disciples!**

This is true in all areas of life. You cannot coach sportspeople by merely assembling them in a lecture hall once a week; you cannot teach the piano to a classroom of thirty students by just sitting them at their desks; you cannot train your children for adulthood by simply having them attend a weekly seminar on family life.

If you're serious about training *anyone* for *anything* – then you need to spend time with them in a small enough group where each person can have personal interaction.

I know a youth pastor who has a weekly Bible class for young people who want to grow as Christians. Thirty to forty teenagers gather each week while he teaches them God's word. Nothing wrong with that! *But you will never train disciples this way!* In addition to helpful Bible teaching like this, there needs to be another opportunity to meet with growing disciples in a smaller setting.

2. You can't grow disciples in a general group

Many churches have a weekly youth group. Maybe ten kids come. Maybe a hundred kids come. This group is usually a mixture of all sorts of kids – from those who are as keen as anything to follow Jesus right through to those who have no interest in following Jesus at all.

Most churches have limited resources. You can't just keep adding more and more activities and meetings into people's crowded diaries. So this question is often asked: *"Can I effectively evangelise non-christians **and** disciple the growing Christians in the same meeting?"*

I have two answers to that question. The first answer is *"Yes, sort of!"* I pray that everything we do in youth ministry will reach both the saved and the unsaved. God's word is active in everyone's life. When I have my absolute core Christians around me and we are working on deep discipling, I will always be aware that there might be someone there whose commitment isn't nearly as strong as they're making out. If I were preaching at a Bible college to those training for ordained ministry, I would still have a slight evangelistic edge to everything I say. Conversely, if I'm sharing a message with non-Christians, I also want to be able to stretch the thinking of those who are already deeply committed.

But my second answer to the question – *"Can I effectively evangelise non-Christians **and** disciple the growing Christians in the same meeting?"* is a more definitive one: *"You might be able to do both, **but you can only do one of them well**"*. That is, you can either evangelise the non-Christians very effectively (and in parentheses, give a little discipleship to the Christians), or, you can disciple the Christians very effectively (and in parentheses, give a little bit of evangelism to the non-Christians). I honestly don't think you can achieve both effectively at the same time.

And here's why: in any youth group meeting (if you want to prevent it from descending into chaos!) you have to pitch your message at the level of *the least interested kids.* That is, you need to make sure that those who are furthest away from Jesus stay interested in what you're saying. Because you know that if you lose their attention, they will cause enough chaos so that nobody learns anything. They are not like polite adult non-Christians who will sit there bored out of their brains, too courteous to interrupt or distract in any way. Teenagers will give you instant feedback on what they think, and if they're getting bored – *they will let you know immediately!*

So it you're trying to achieve both effective evangelism **and** deep discipling in the one meeting, you will most likely end up with one of the following two outcomes:

1. You will pitch your message at the least interested kids – which could well result in effective evangelism. But there will be little deep discipleship for the really committed kids.

2. You will keep pitching your message at the committed kids – which *could* result in deep discipleship – but more likely will result in bad behaviour as you lose the interest of those on the fringe. Eventually, these 'fringers' will stop coming – then you *do* have the possibility of achieving deep discipleship – but only because the non-Christians have stopped attending! And then, of course, you can't do any effective evangelism!

3. You need to meet with growing disciples separately

Even if you run a general youth group, and then subdivide into small groups as part of that meeting (which is not a bad way to run a youth group!), I don't believe you will achieve deep discipleship with those students who really want to grow. At some stage you need to meet with the growing disciples *separately from meeting with everyone else.*

I discovered this from bitter experience. We used to run Bible-study groups for our students. They all met on Sunday afternoon in the church hall. We met together – sang together – had some up-front Bible teaching – and then spent the remainder of the time in Bible-study groups.

We would finish with dinner together, and then head off to church together. (*If you're running a programme like this, there's nothing essentially wrong with it!*) But here's what we found: *we weren't really training disciples for a world-changing ministry!* We were having Bible studies about discipleship. Pitched at a group where everyone was welcome. The interested and the not-so-interested. We were teaching the Bible. We were doing "small-d" discipling. *But we weren't equipping disciples to change the world!*

I honestly believe that if you genuinely want to transform new believers into world-changing disciples, then *you need to meet with them separately from the general crowd.* You need to find those who *genuinely* want to grow as disciples, and separate them from everyone else so that you can disciple them at a deep level. You need to take aside those who want to learn more.

4. How do you find the right ones?

a) Pray: Pray that God will raise up those who want to learn more. Ask God to help you select those whom He knows are ready to go deeper.

b) Challenge: Keep challenging those who come to your general youth group that there is far more to following Jesus than can be presented at your normal group. Challenge them that you are looking for people who want to be trained to go and change the world.

c) Invite: Invite those whom God has specifically laid on your heart. Talk with them about the potential you see in them. Challenge them about the possibility of going further. Cast before them your vision of faithful young disciples who are passionate to win the world for Christ one life at a time.

d) Don't make it too easy: This might seem like a strange idea. But don't make it too easy for people to join your discipleship group. Here's why: *you don't want to simply reproduce the "general" crowd you get at your normal youth group!* You want to identify and separate those who are really keen to grow as disciples.

They need to know that their discipling group is a top-level commitment. They need to know that preparation will need to be done. They need to know that there may be memory verses to learn. They need to know that they are meeting for a time of solid Bible study, where they will be held accountable for their growth.

Once I had some boys in Year 10 who had recently made commitments to follow Jesus. I invited them to join a discipleship group where they could be trained to change the world for Jesus. We could not find a convenient time, so we met Wednesday mornings at 7 am in the party room of the local McDonald's. One boy used to leave home at 6 am and walk in the dark to get to the group. By not making it too easy to attend, we sorted out the ones who were really serious!

e) **Help Christians work out if they're ready:** The danger in setting a high standard is that you can end up with a discipleship group that looks like an exclusive club. Only for the insiders. Only for the favoured ones. This is certainly not the end result that you're after!

So rather than acting like a spiritual bouncer and saying, *"You can't come in because I don't think you're ready"*, you're better off getting students to **exclude themselves**. That is, by being up-front about the high level of commitment that you need to have, you can help students work out *for themselves* whether they're ready to join.

If I have someone who wants to join a discipleship group, but has never given any evidence that they're a Christian and keen to grow, then I might help them sort out whether this is the right step by checking with them the commitment that is necessary:

- *"Do you realise that this is a top-priority group – which means you're making a commitment to be there every single week? And if for any reason you can't make it, you'll need to notify your leader beforehand?"*

- *"You understand that there may be homework for you to do before you attend the group? And there may well be Bible verses you'll be required to memorise?"*

- *"You do know that its an hour and a half of Bible study? There are no games, no activities – all we do is learn from the Bible how to follow Jesus."*

If they seem happy to agree to all this (even though I don't think they're ready), I will use it as an opportunity to talk about their commitment.

- *"You understand that this group is designed for those who are keen Christians. Tell me a little about how you became a Christian."*

In the end, if they are ready to keep all the commitments that we require, then even if I think they're not ready, I may well let them join a group *on the understanding that we don't lower our standards to accommodate them.* In a recent discipleship group that I led for Year 7 boys – one boy started with us even though he was fairly clear in his mind that he wasn't ready to commit his life to Jesus. But he was happy to explore the claims of Jesus along with his friends, and he stayed with us for two years before he decided that Jesus was wanting a commitment from him that he wasn't prepared to give.

f) **Offer a "first step" before the final commitment:** We try to start all our groups with a 5-week *Discovering Jesus* course. It's a 5-week commitment that takes students through the gospel. It's a way of helping them work out whether they really are prepared to follow Jesus or not. By making the 5-week *Discovering Jesus* course an entry requirement for our discipleship groups, we create another filter to help sort out those who are indeed ready for deep discipleship.

5. How do you programme this?

How do you add an extra discipleship group into your normal schedule without overloading everyone's diaries? Here are some suggestions:

a) **Meeting one-on-one:** If you decide to meet one-on-one with someone you are going to disciple, you will have amazing flexibility. You can find a time and location that suits you both. This can often be a good way forward, especially in discipling adults. At our church we encourage our discipleship leaders to have some one-on-one contact with each young person, but with teenagers we don't recommend it as the *primary* method. Here's why:

- We never have enough adult leaders to disciple everyone one-on-one. It works better for us to have each leader with a small group.

- Teenagers can sometimes feel intimidated when meeting one-on-one with an adult.

- I think young Christians open up more *and* learn more when they interact with their peers. I have found that encouragement from their peers is one of the key elements in helping high-schoolers. I would far prefer to disciple a young person in a small group with friends of their own age.

- In today's era of suspicion, there are legal and

social reasons why we need to be *very careful* in working one-on-one with those aged under 18. Not all parents would be happy with this arrangement! Indeed, your own church might have guidelines which would rule this out as an option.

b) **The weekly home group:** This is the way we currently do things. In addition to expecting a young Christian to be at church on Sunday to learn and grow; and in addition to expecting a young Christian to show up at our youth group on Friday night so they can minister to the non-Christians who are there, we also expect a high-school disciple to belong to one of our *Discipleship Teams*. These are Bible-study groups that meet in homes at a time and location to suit the participants. Normally one adult leader with around 6-8 young Christians.

The particulars for these groups are not advertised in our programme. That means you can't *just show up* at one. You need to ask first!

By having them located in people's homes, with each group deciding their own time and date, everything is more flexible and easier to accommodate in a busy week. Also, a reasonable percentage of our groups meet just before or after our youth group, or just before or after church. This means they have two commitments per week rather than three.

This is a good programme to get both effective evangelism *and* effective discipleship accomplished. The main negative is that it gives you a very busy programme! But you don't have to add in an extra group like this. Here is another way to accomplish the same goal *without adding in any extra timeslots*…

c) **The fortnightly model:** This won't accomplish results as quickly as the above model, but it will achieve your goals when resources are scarce. Simply drop your weekly youth group programme back to fortnightly. Then on the *off* week, you have your small groups in people's homes. Once again, the details of these are not advertised in your programme. To the outside world, it simply looks as if you have a fortnightly youth group. But for those who are keen to learn more, there is the opportunity for deep discipleship every other week.

There are negatives to this programme:

- By cutting your youth group back to fortnightly, you will have less momentum in your programming. You will probably have fewer people attending; they will get out of the habit of coming every week; and they may have difficulty remembering which week it's on.

- Fortnightly discipleship groups will travel at half the pace of weekly ones.

But this is not a bad approach to programming where your personnel resources are limited and diary dates are crowded. But ideally, I want to meet separately with growing disciples *every week*.

It's up to you *how* you do it. But if you want to be serious about training a whole new generation of believers, work out a way to meet with those keen disciples separately from ministering to everyone else. In the next chapter, we'll look at *what to do* once you gather your disciples together.

Chapter 11

Making your discipleship group work

Okay – you've found some keen Christians – you're ready to get started. You've agreed on a date and time – and you're all set to go. Here are some key issues that will help ensure your discipleship group really works.

1. Have Christians who *want* to be discipled

If you really want to make disciples, you need to make sure that the group you have assemled actually *wants to be discipled.* There might be many reasons why students say *"yes"* to your gracious invitation to join your group. Perhaps they want to be with their best friends. Perhaps they really like you as a leader. Perhaps they don't want to feel left out. They need to know why they're there. They need to be teachable. They need to be inspired by you.

2. Keep parents informed

When you're working with young people under 18, it really matters that you keep parents informed every step of the way. You need to have voice contact with them before the group starts – and make sure that you give them written information with exact time, location, and contact details. Ongoing information to parents will head off possible disruptions. This particularly matters when your young people have parents who do not attend your church.

3. Get everyone ready for the first meeting

You really want to set the pace with your first meeting. So it's worth taking the extra effort to make sure that the first time you meet is indeed the model you want to continue. As well as the written information that lets them know all the details, make some phone calls during the lead-up week to ensure that everyone is right for kick-off!

- *Ensure that **everyone** shows up at the first meeting.*
- *Sort out any transport hassles.*
- *Make sure everyone brings what they will need (e.g. Bible, pen, etc).*

By the way, I think it's a good idea that everyone brings their own Bible and their own pen and anything else that's needed. It helps set the tone that 'what we're doing is serious'. This is no different from any other group they belong to. If they have a commitment to a sporting team, then they need to bring their uniform and other gear to every match and every practice. Get them in the habit early!

4. Choose your location carefully

I think the ideal location is in someone's home. If you want to rotate homes, then keep the same home for a school-term, and then change to another for the next term. (If you change the location every week, people will find it too hard to keep track of where you are!)

Homes also have the advantage of being cosier than a church hall. I have run discipleship groups in both locations, and the atmosphere of a lounge room has always led to more in-depth conversations than the starkness of a church hall!

Maybe a church hall is your only option. But I would think that if there is the possibility of using someone's home, you will be better off. Using a home also keeps your group more private – you are less likely to have someone just show up and say: *"Can I join in?"*

One more reason why I like homes: the parents get to see a little of what you do. They get to meet you – meet all the others – and are more likely to be active in their support for you. I especially like to meet in a home where the parents are not Christians. Many parents have started attending our church because they have seen changes happening in their teenager!

Wherever you meet, make sure that the room that you're in is reasonably private. You don't want any through-traffic or people overhearing what your group members are sharing confidentially! A lounge room with a door that can be closed is ideal.

5. Think about your refreshments

I like the idea of having refreshments available at some stage. But make sure that the refreshments do not interrupt your work of discipling. I favour either having the refreshments right at the beginning, or right at the end – and not having them available while the group is meeting. A large box of yummy donuts can prove to be a distraction if kept open during a Bible study!

My *favourite* way to have refreshments is to have them right at the beginning **and then take them away at a specified time**. This has a number of advantages:

- *It gives your participants an added incentive to be on time.*

- *The munchies are available as people walk in – which encourages people to congregate and start chatting to each other.*
- *It allows for small variations in the arrival time of members.*
- *It means that those who arrive late miss out!*

I had a Year 12 boys' discipleship group that met every Sunday afternoon at 4 pm. After our group we would have a bite to eat, and then head on to church together. We had what we called "the 4 o'clock chocs". That is, at 4 pm, a selection of chocolates was brought out – to be available as people arrived. We would pass them around as we chatted. **But at 4:10 pm the chocolates were taken away!** I had one boy who was *always* late. He went for some months without ever realising that we had "the 4 o'clock chocs" **because he was never there when they were out!**

6. Set the vision

The first time you meet, set the vision for why you're meeting. Remind people of the big vision that you want to achieve. Say it loud and long the first time you meet – and keep repeating it down the track whenever it's needed. One of the sure ways for discipleship to be derailed is when the group members lose sight of the big picture and just focus on the weekly meeting. **Remember, your aim is not to have a weekly discipleship meeting; your aim is to train disciples who will transform this world for Jesus.**

You need to work out your own vision. And you need to work out how to communicate it effectively. It may well include some of the following ingredients:

- *"We're meeting because we want to equip each other*

to go and make a difference for Jesus."

- *"This group really matters because it's going to help us go and win our friends to following Jesus."*
- *"This group will enable each one of us to stand strongly for Jesus no matter what we face."*
- *"By supporting each other as brothers or sisters in Christ, we make sure that not one of us ever has to walk alone."*
- *"This is the place to grow as a Christian. This is the place to get stronger in your faith. This is your main support group to help you continue strongly as Christ's person on this planet all the days of your life."*

Can you see how this is a very different vision from *"We meet to study the Bible and pray"?* Yes – we do pray and study the Bible when we meet, but we do those things for a purpose – that we might be effectively trained as Christ's disciples so that we can make a difference to this planet.

The test of how well your group is going won't be whether your members enjoy the warm fellowship that they experience. The success of your group will be measured by:

- *how your group members go at standing obediently for Jesus throughout the rest of their lives.*
- *how your group members go at winning their world to Jesus one life at a time.*

Set this vision before them – and keep it there so it lasts for a lifetime.

7. Set the values

For a discipleship group to work well, everyone in it needs

to agree on the *values* that you will all adhere to. If different group members have *different values* from each other, they will treat the group in their own way, and this will lead to ongoing frustration. You need to set the standard with these values – but you need to help *all group members* to agree to them. You are the coach – it's okay for the coach to set the standard for their team. Don't be scared to ask for a big commitment – teenagers are easily capable of rising to the occasion!

Here are some of the values you might want to work into your group:

a) **Top priority:** This simply means that of all the things you do in a week, your discipleship group is in the very highest category. That means you rearrange other things in your week to make way for it. That means you wouldn't miss a week without an exceptional reason. Students aren't in control of every decision they make – they have parents and schools who will sometimes make those decisions for them. But wherever possible, your discipleship group needs to be seen by all members as *top priority*.

b) **No unexplained absences:** This follows from having the group as *top priority*. If for some reason any member cannot attend, they must notify their leader beforehand. You never want to have a situation where your group is meeting, and someone says, *"Where's Fred?"* and everyone just shrugs their shoulders. Nothing will debilitate a group more than having unexplained absences. By the way, this is not an extraordinarily high standard. When I coach my junior soccer team, I have exactly the same standard. Every player knows, if they miss training without notifying me first, they will sit on the bench for the game. Let's keep our discipleship standards *at least as high* as local sporting coaches!

c) **We work together as a team:** This simply means that when there's something we're meant to be doing, *we all do it.* When it's time to pray, we all do it. When it's time to memorise a Bible verse, we all do it. When it's time to sit and listen, we all do it. When it's time to clean up, we all do it. That is the essence of a team. We work together. We sacrifice our own personal interests for the good of the whole body.

d) **We respect each other:** This can be a steep learning curve for adolescents. But if we have a discipleship team without respect, we have a recipe for disaster. *Respecting each other* could mean things like:

- *Everyone gets listened to. That would mean not talking when someone else is talking. Not interrupting, not distracting, not being inattentive. We honour each other by valuing each person's contribution.*

- *Everyone gets taken seriously. Don't turn somebody's contribution into a joke. Don't make fun of each other.*

- *Everyone gets included. Don't have conversations or activities that exclude.*

- *We use words that encourage. We don't put each other down. We don't insult each other. We lift each other up with our words.*

e) **We maintain confidentiality:** Personal things that are shared in the group are kept confidential in the group. Everyone needs to agree on this. Otherwise people will not be honest. It's okay to tell someone outside the group what *you* said in the group, but you need to ask the other person's permission before you share anything that *anyone else* said.

f) **We're honest with each other:** Once you have established the value of *confidentiality*, you can then establish the value of *honesty*. Your discipleship group is not a place for pretending. It's okay to fail – and it's okay to be honest about it. We want to be a group where there is love and acceptance of each other – even when we fail. It is only by being *honest* that we can hold each other *accountable*.

g) **We hold each other accountable:** No-one walks alone. That's the core value that makes discipling work. We care so much for each other that we do not allow each other to wander away. We are not here to judge each other; we are not here to condemn each other; but we are here to walk with each other as brothers and sisters. We do not have private sins and private commitments. When any of us makes a decision to change an area of our life, we have a loving support group who will hold us accountable to keep that change.

h) **Membership by invitation only:** What you don't want is members just bringing "any old friend" to sit in on your group. If you're going to build confidentiality and honesty, your group can't have a constantly changing membership. If anyone would like to invite a new member to the group – then they bring that suggestion to the group and you all agree on it before it happens.

i) **We always want to reach others:** The danger in having *"membership by invitation only"* is that your discipling group can end up being very inward looking. All group members need to understand that the *reason you exist* is so that others can be reached with the message of Jesus. One of the signs that your discipleship group is effective is that every group member is continually active in reaching their friends for Christ.

8. Set the behaviour standards

When you're working with adolescents, it's important that you all agree on the behaviour standards so that the group can operate successfully. You don't want discipline problems to derail your discipleship goal!

I would normally do this by getting students to fill in and sign a commitment sheet. I would then keep those signed commitment sheets available should I need to refer an individual student back to them at a later date. Apart from each student having the opportunity to write their name on the sheet, and date it and sign it, I would ask them for written answers to finish the following statements:

- *Why I want to join this group:*
- *What I hope our group really achieves:*
- *Here's what I will do to help our group really work:*
- *Here's what should happen if I am distracting our group from really growing:*

I would have the students read out their answers and discuss them. You may need to guide the discussion with your wisdom, but it would be good for you all to agree on behaviour standards. Especially *"Here's what should happen if I am distracting our group from really growing"*. Sometimes students will be very harsh on themselves. But it's important for them to see – there will be consequences for disruptive behaviour.

As a guideline, here are some suggestions for what the consequences *might* be for disruptive behaviour *(this will vary greatly depending on the age and maturity of your students)*:

- *The leader will warn a student once that their behaviour is unacceptable.*

- *The next warning, the leader will let the student know that they are on the verge of being excluded from the group to have some "time out".*

- *If a student continues, they will be asked to sit outside the group (maybe in the next room) to take some "time out" and calm down.*

- *The student can then ask to be re-admitted on the condition that they behave properly.*

- *This then gives you a chance to talk with the student individually after the group.*

Once again, there is nothing particularly strict about these guidelines. When I had young adolescents in my football team, if they were disruptive while I was coaching, I would apply the same standards. The important thing is that you *agree on what the standards are – and get everyone's agreement and commitment to that standard.*

9. Be pastoral

Don't get so focused on "getting the study finished" that you overlook the real pastoral needs of each of your students. When you meet, ask each of your students how their week has gone. If one of them tells your group about some difficulties that they are having, then that is a good time to pause and look after them in your community of care.

Some suggestions:

- *Don't just dismiss their comment and move on.*
- *Listen to what they're saying.*
- *Resist the temptation to simply give advice.*
- *Support them in what they're saying.*
- *Offer practical help.*
- *Get the whole group involved in praying for them.*
- *Teach your group that all of us get hurt at sometime, and it's okay to talk about it.*
- *Remind your group of the need to keep confidentiality within the group. Personal sharing in your group shouldn't end up as gossip!*
- *If caring for a particular situation is beyond you, then with the permission of the student concerned, involve someone at your church who is more senior and experienced than you.*

You're now about ready to roll. So what are you going to teach them?

Chapter 12

Three key steps for a new disciple

Okay – you've assembled your group – you've started on your journey. What will you teach them? What do they need?

I think there are three key needs for any growing disciple. However you do it, you need to cover this material thoroughly so it becomes "second nature" for the new believer. [1]

1. Understand your new life

A person who has become a Christian has undergone the biggest change in their life. They have moved from being God's enemy to God's friend; they have moved from being a rebel to a worshipper; they have moved from being an outcast to being God's own child; they have moved from the kingdom of darkness into the kingdom of light; they have moved from being slaves of sin to slaves of righteousness; they have moved from eternal death to eternal life.

This is a big change! The growing disciple needs to understand this change, and to have the reality of it re-inforced. They will have all sorts of doubts; they will have all sorts of questions.

---

1. These concepts are spelled out in far more detail in *Discipleship Training* (see bibliography). There is also a more detailed synopsis in Appendix 1.

a) **Knowing what's happened:** The new disciple needs to be taken through what has actually happened to them. They may need to go through the basics of the gospel to be reminded of what Jesus' death and resurrection have really achieved.

b) **Being reassured:** One of the key fears of the new Christian will be: *"Is it all really true? Has God really accepted me? Am I really a Christian? Am I truly forgiven?"* You need to take the new believer to those sections of the Bible which will address these very real fears.

c) **Knowing God's protection:** New believers are vulnerable to the attacks of the evil one. There are temptations at every corner for the new believer to turn back to their old ways. They need to understand the attacks of the devil, and know the promises of God, who will protect them.

d) **Living the new life:** There is a whole world of growth for a new believer. There is a whole new life to be discovered, learned, lived and celebrated. Realising how to put their new faith into action in every area of their life will demand a lot of every new believer. Part of our ongoing journey with them will be to walk with them in many of these areas, and equip them to continue on in faithful obedience.[2]

e) **Making godly decisions:** Not every area of life can be

---

2. Most of the content of living this new life can be found in Chapter 13.

covered in a disciple's training. They have a lifetime in front of them of having to make wise and godly choices. As they get to know God better, they will start to make decisions which reflect the character of God. Each disciple needs to learn how to make these decisions – how to make wise decisions – how to make godly decisions – how to make obedient decisions.

The basis for this is understanding how Jesus is Lord over *every* aspect of your life. Disciples will make more and more godly decisions as their understanding of Jesus being *Lord* moves from the theoretical to the practical. Knowing how God guides will help them to make godly decisions. God knows us intimately and knows what's best for us. So the choices he wants us to make are the *best* choices for our life!

The key here for a discipleship trainer is not necessarily just to give the right answers to every question a growing disciple asks, but to point the disciple towards the biblical truths that will help them *to work it out for themselves*. Every disciple is going to have to spend a lifetime making decisions – quite likely about issues that have never occurred to us! Equipping a disciple to be godly in their wisdom is a skill that will last them for life!

2. Understand your God

Every disciple needs to know God better. We must discover his character as revealed in the Scriptures. If we're saying that we're going to live our whole life devoted to God, then we need to get to know him! Because, as we discover his character, we get to know who he is and how he acts. And when we go deeper into knowing God, then we can go deeper in responding to him the way he wants.

I have a personal confession at this point. When I first tried to assemble a training list of everything that you would want to teach a new disciple, I left this point out completely! I remember doing an analysis of my completed training list, and discovering I had five studies about the Bible, **but not one study about God!** *(How embarrassing! What an evangelical blind spot!).*

There are three key ways that God has revealed himself to us:

i) Knowing God as our Father

God firstly reveals himself as our Father. There are two key aspects of this which every disciple needs to understand:

- *He is the mighty creator – all powerful, all holy and there is no-one like him.*
- *He loves us dearly with the tender love of a father.*

George had trouble believing all this. He was okay with understanding that God was almighty, all-powerful, and all-judging, but he really hesitated when we talked about God the Father loving him as a precious child.

As we chatted further, George revealed a little bit about his own family background. His own father had never wanted him. His own father was often drunk, often angry, often violent. For him to understand God the Father as a God of *absolute love* was a difficult step. It was completely outside his range of comprehension. And yet as we guided George more and more to understanding the biblical love of his heavenly Father, there was a huge breakthrough in his life. Rather than obeying God out of a reluctant sense of *fear,* he now obeyed God as a joyful response to being *a loved and precious child.*

ii) Knowing Jesus as our Lord

This aspect of God's character is crucial. Every disciple signs up to follow Christ. He is the one we really need to get to know. He is the one who takes us to his Father and sends us his Spirit. Three key issues about Jesus to focus on with any disciple:

- *He is fully God – the promised Messiah – the Lord of all.*
- *He is the Servant-King who died and rose for us.*
- *He will return to judge the living and the dead.*

Let me pause for a moment. I don't want you to get the impression that Jesus' death and resurrection are just bullet points on a list. For in his sacrificial death and his glorious resurrection, Jesus shows us the very heart of God. At the cross and resurrection we see the judgment of God and the love of God. We start to comprehend the horror of sin and the fullness of forgiveness. We tremble at the reality of hell and marvel at Jesus' victory over the devil, sin and death. We experience the miracle that enables any one of us to have a full, free and intimate relationship with the Lord of the universe.

> **Romans 4:25** *"He was delivered over to death for our sins and was raised to life for our justification."*

You cannot spend too much time helping a growing disciple to understand how central Jesus' death and resurrection really are. They are the absolute basis for our faith; they are the only certainty of our future. If you want to teach the character of God, Jesus' death and resurrection are the starting point, the central foundation and the final culmination. The victory of Jesus in his death and resurrection **is** the victory for every disciple.

> Louise was a new Christian at our church. A faithful and obedient young lady, but she appeared to have difficulty in really trusting God. She believed in God; she had committed her life to God; but she appeared reluctant to confess personal issues to God.
>
> As we chatted further, it became evident where the blockage was: *she felt that God was still angry with her!* She was worried about bringing her sins before God because she was worried that God would be so disappointed with her, and might punish her for her failings.
>
> What a joy to be able to share with her that God's anger for her sin *had already been poured out on Jesus!* She no longer had to try and "make up for her sins" because *Jesus had already done it!*

Do not underestimate the need to keep bringing new disciples back to the cross of Jesus. For it's only when they know the power of *full forgiveness* that they will be able to respond with *full obedience*.

iii) Knowing God's Spirit as our powerful helper

The miracle of following God is that God himself lives in us. God's Holy Spirit has been given to every believer that we might know for certain the great truths of God. God's Spirit takes God's word and applies it to our lives. God's Spirit takes us into the very relationships that exist within the Godhead – so that, by the power of the Spirit, we live out the submission that God the Son has to God the Father, and we receive all the blessings that God the Father lavishes on God the Son.

There are three key activities of God's Holy Spirit in the New Testament, and every believer needs to understand these and live by them:

- *God's Spirit is given to every believer – to live in them, assure them, and actively guide them.*

- *God's Spirit will keep changing us to be more and more like Jesus.*

- *God's Spirit will equip us for ministry to others.*

3. Understand your new mission [3]

One vital key to helping a disciple to power on as Christ's follower is helping them to understand that *Jesus has enlisted them for his ministry team.* Jesus has a job for them to do. Not a "once-off" job, but a lifetime task – *to go and make other disciples.*

It is so crucial that a new disciple understands this right at the outset. You want to establish this lifetime habit right from the word go. That's why, in our *Discipleship Training* Series, lessons about *your mission* are right there in the introductory book – in lessons 2, 3 and 4.

---

3. Further details in Chapter 18.

New disciples need to understand these two key biblical concepts:

> i. *The church is the community of God's people, where we are called on to serve each other in love.*
>
> ii. *The church is God's main strategy to spread his message so that many more will believe.*

In each of these two concepts, each believer has a vital role to fulfil so that we encourage our fellow-believers, and reach out to those who do not yet know Jesus. This leads to the two key aspects to understanding our mission here on planet earth:

> i. *We are stewards or managers of God's great gifts, and our job is to use whatever God has given us to bless others.*
>
> ii. *We are witnesses for Jesus – we get to tell others about the magnificent things he has done so that they can become disciples as well.*

These are the three concepts that every disciple needs to grab hold of: understand your new life; understand your God; understand your new mission. Once you have introduced a growing disciple to these key concepts, you then need to teach them the Bible so that they develop the lasting habits of growth. *(Next chapter!)*

Chapter 13

Teaching the six habits of growth

God has designed a whole new way for us to live – and grow! As a trainer, you need to drill the growing disciple in the essential habits of growth. If you can establish consistency in these habits, then you will produce a lifelong, growing disciple who will not remain dependent on you for every step.

I have summarised the six habits of growth so that they spell out the word **G–R–O–W–T–H**. Here they are in summary:

G   **G**athering with Christians

R   **R**eaching others

O   **O**beying Jesus

W   **W**illing to give

T   **T**alking with God

H   **H**earing God speak.

For further detail, please read this in conjunction with the information in the "Discipleship Training" Series (see bibliography), which contains detailed instructions on how to teach the basics of growth. I have not reproduced all that information here. A more detailed outline of this course can also be found in Appendix 1.

1. Gathering with Christians

The new believer will find their greatest support from the fellowship and teamwork of other Christians. Far and above everything else, this is the one key factor which will most likely determine whether they stay on track or not. A growing disciple who is plugged into meeting together with other Christians – both in a large group, and a small group – will find all the support they need when the going gets tough.

There are two key areas I want to plug every disciple into so they have a rich experience of *gathering with Christians.*

a) **In their small group:** This is absolutely crucial. Every disciple needs to be in a group where they will be held accountable for their walk with Jesus. This will probably be their number one support group for the rest of their life.

b) **At church:** While a small group will provide the intimate sharing and relationships that are needed, each disciple also needs to be planted in a wider congregation. They need to learn to worship with all ages. They need to be challenged by direct preaching. They need to learn to praise and worship God in the assembly of his people.

The Bible never makes the distinction between the *small group* and the *big group.* But here's what I have found over the years. From time to time we have young people who are genuine Christians, who are plugged into their small group, but, for one reason or another, *never get involved in church.* Conversely, some of our young Christians get plugged in at church, but never settle into an effective small group. While biblically it would be hard to make a case that either of these groups were doing anything wrong, my observation is that *students who don't get involved in **both** church on Sunday **and** in their small group rarely keep going as faithful disciples!*

Alan was a great kid who attended our youth group. He seemed interested, but he had never taken the step of attending church or planting himself in a small group.

"Do you have to go to church to be a Christian?" he asked me one day. I replied: *"Do you have to join a football team to be a footballer?"*

He looked at me with the exasperated eyes of a person who wasn't going to accept defeat easily. *"Of course you can be a footballer without joining a football team. You can get registered; you can wear the uniform; you can buy a ball; you can practise in your backyard. Technically you're a footballer – you don't have to join a team!"*

"You may be technically correct," I replied. *"You probably can be a footballer without joining a football team. But here are some key questions to think through: Will you ever be a **good** footballer? Will you ever really **enjoy** being a footballer? And more importantly – how long do you think you will **last** as a footballer?"*

He nodded knowingly at this. He started attending church that week!

Nobody lasts by themselves. If you want to transform new believers into world-changing disciples, you must ensure that they are firmly planted in a body of believers who will support them all the way.

2. Reaching others

The flip-side of the importance of gathering with Christians is to reach out to non-Christians. Every disciple needs to understand that Jesus has called them to be a *"fisher of men"*. [1] Here's why this is a crucial ministry for disciples to understand **right from the very start**.

- *Being a disciple means they are also a disciple-maker.* [2] *There is no distinction in the Bible between the two. It is a crafty invention of the devil to convince Christians that* **"you're only a disciple – other people are meant to do the ministry"**.

- *New people bring new people. You will find that new converts are often the absolute best at inviting new people to hear about Jesus. They're so excited about their new life that they haven't yet learned to be a lazy Christian!*

3. Obeying Jesus

The growing disciple needs to understand that Christianity is not just a belief system – *it is meant to lead to a changed life!* The biblical emphasis is this: God has made you a new person, therefore there is a whole new life to lead. [3] Probably the longest lesson that a disciple will need to learn is that of having a whole life which is in submission

---

1. Matthew 4:18-20. This concept is discussed in more detail in Chapter 18.
2. Matthew 4:18-20 – again!
3. Ephesians 4:22-24

to Jesus by obeying him. Once they have conquered a particular aspect, they will discover that there is a whole new area of obedience that they need to learn!

You and your growing disciple will need to keep each other on the cutting edge of obedience. Joyful obedience. If you have established the values of **honesty** and **accountability**, then you can sharpen each other for ongoing obedience. To help a growing disciple understand solid obedience, then you need to help them also understand **repentance, confession** and **forgiveness**.

4. Willing to give

God is a totally giving God and he wants his people to be just like him. Generosity is one of the hallmarks of a faithful disciple. For anyone who genuinely loves others will show this by their giving nature. *You can give without loving, but you cannot love without giving.*

Every disciple needs to be willing to give of themselves – to give of their whole life for the sake of the kingdom. But here are three areas where all disciples need to be specifically challenged in their giving:

- **a) Time:** Disciples need to be willing to use their time to glorify God and bless his people.

- **b) Talents:** We need to use our God-given ministry gifts to serve each other and build God's church.

- **c) Treasure:** We all need to be challenged to be generous in giving away what God has entrusted to us. We are called to be stewards who bless others with God's resources. Our attitude to our money and possessions will be a key indicator of how our heart is really going.

Mark was in Year 8, and was sitting next to me at church. We had recently been studying generosity in our Discipleship Team, and he was watching the offertory plate as it made its way down the rows towards him. He was thinking about whether he could afford to give anything from his meagre resources.

I'm not quite sure what came over him, but as the offertory bowl passed him, he turned his wallet upside down and shook it vigorously so that a small number of coins fell out.

At the end of the service, I asked him about how he was feeling about his giving. *"I just wanted to give everything!"* he said. So I asked him, *"Was that difficult for you to do?"* He replied *"No – I feel really good about doing that!"*

Then he thought a little further. *"But it didn't really amount to much. There was probably less than $5 there. What difference would that make?"*

I reminded him that his younger brother had just become a Christian. *"Do you remember that 'New Christians Pack' that we gave your younger brother? That cost about $5. Your generosity has just paid to help your brother grow as Christian."*

But here's what delighted my heart. It wasn't the *amount* that he had given. It was the simple truth that he was developing a *generous heart.* You can always be sure that your attitude toward your money and possessions will *always* be a key indicator to the state of your heart!

Matthew 6:21 *"For where your treasure is, there your heart will be also."*

5. Talking with God

Prayer is the lifeblood of every believer. Listen to the words of Jesus:

John 15:5 *"apart from me you can do nothing."*

For any disciple to learn and grow, they need to understand that prayer is their constant lifeline. They need to depend on God and come humbly before him on every issue. A growing disciple needs to be more than a *person who prays*; they need to become a *person of prayer*. By praying with a growing disciple, and teaching and modelling for them how to approach God boldly – and yet with trembling – you will sow into them a pattern of life that will stand them strong through every test.

Every disciple will want to develop an ongoing passion for prayer when they are by themselves, and also when they are gathered with other Christians. They will want to rejoice in organised times where they devote themselves to prayer, as well as the spontaneous times where they will simply cry out to God. Prayer *is* the constant drum-beat for living as a disciple. It is not an *added-on extra* that just gets squeezed in at the end! *(So make sure your discipleship group doesn't treat it this way!)*

It's interesting the question that Jesus' disciples asked him when they wanted him to disciple them:

> **Luke 11:1** *"One day Jesus was praying in a certain place. When he finished, one of his disciples said to him, "Lord, teach us to pray, just as John taught his disciples."*

The disciples were well aware how masters would train their followers. They had observed how John the Baptist worked with his disciples. Their request to Jesus wasn't *"Show us how to obey you!"* or *"Can you teach us how to read the Bible",* but they simply asked: *"Lord, teach us to pray, just as John taught his disciples."*

I love my evangelical heritage and I have much to thank my brothers and sisters for because they have taught me to have a love of God's word. But I fear that from my own tradition, Bible-reading has been emphasised at the expense of prayer. Both matter; both are vital; they are two sides of the same conversation. If you can teach other disciples to pray – and model for them a life of prayer – then you will stand them in good stead in living a whole lifetime that depends absolutely on entrusting everything to God.

6. Hearing God speak

God's Holy Spirit is active in bringing God's word to our hearts. We want to develop disciples who are open and sensitive to the leading of the Holy Spirit. God's Spirit can speak to us in many different ways. But the place where God has *promised* to speak is in his written word – the Bible.

We want our growing disciples to be people of the Bible. To read God's word. To trust God's word. To obey God's word. To live God's word. Christianity isn't based on having opinions about God – it's based on God revealing himself through his written word – the Bible.

There are three key areas to help a growing disciple to become a person of God's word:

a) **Regular personal time with God:** Of utmost importance is to help a growing disciple to have their own regular, daily time with God – when they simply read his word and cry out to him in prayer. Just hanging out with God *one-on-one*. This is such a vital habit. You should model this for your growing disciples: do it together with them; release them to be able to do it by themselves; *and then hold each other accountable that you keep doing it faithfully.* Of all the Christians I have known who have become less enthusiastic in their faith, when you ask the question: *"How are you going in your own personal time with God?",* you quickly discover that this is one of the first discipleship habits to go.

b) **Memorising verses[4]:** This aspect of discipleship is easy to neglect in our hi-tech world with modern education methods. But I have found that memorising verses has been one of the most helpful things to my own Christian growth – and I know it has been a similar blessing to many disciples I have taught Scripture memorising to. Here's the value of scripture memory: *you know for certain what God's mind is on a particular matter.* You can then use God's word to teach and correct yourself; and you can use God's word to encourage others.

---

4. See more details in Chapter 19.

c) **Learning from Bible teachers:** As well as their personal time with God, and their personal Scripture memory, you want each growing disciple to be open to learning from those God has gifted to teach his word. Your own attitude will be the key here! You need to help other disciples to have teachable hearts so that they will soak in good Bible-teaching at every opportunity.

- When they're studying God's word in your small group.

- When they're listening to the sermon at church.

- When they're learning from Christian conferences, books, messages on DVD, CD, MP3 or podcast – or one of the many other forms of media that can be used to teach God's word.

I believe that these are the six key areas where growing disciples need to have the bulk of their training. Model these concepts; teach these concepts; and inspire other disciples to live an entire lifetime that is devoted to continually growing in their relationship with God.

Being a discipleship leader

SECTION 4

Chapter 14
The discipling relationship

Over my years of ministry, the absolute key to transforming new believers into world-changing disciples is the relationship between the disciple and the discipler. If there's one element that you want to get right – this is it. This matters more than the curriculum you study; it matters more than the activities you plan; it matters more than the advice you give. If you're planning to enter a relationship where you help bring a growing disciple to maturity, then you are entering a very privileged relationship. The integrity of this relationship matters above all else.

Here's why!

1. It's a reproducing relationship

I'm not quite sure who said it first – but the following quote has the ring of truth: "*You teach what you know, but you reproduce what you are.*" In the end it's not the amount of knowledge you have that will be the determining factor. Making a disciple isn't primarily about imparting information into another person. And deep down, it's not your personality. Making a disciple isn't mainly about injecting your social skills into another person. The absolute key issue that matters far and beyond everything else for someone who is a discipler – is their Christlike character. Because, in the end, what you impart into a growing disciple is your **heart**.

Of all the things you will read in this book, this is the most important. The absolute determining factor in how well you can transform a new believer into a world-changing disciple will be the state of your heart. Yes, that's right, **your** heart – not **their** heart! **Because, whatever is in your heart will be transferred into theirs!**

Listen to the words of Jesus:

> **Luke 6:40** *"A student is not above his teacher, but everyone who is fully trained will be like his teacher."*

The Greek word for "student" is exactly the same word that means "disciple".[1] So this verse is telling us that when a disciple is fully trained, they will be just like their teacher. If you are training someone else to be a disciple of Jesus, they will end up following him **just as you do!** They will pick up your strengths – they will copy your achievements – **and they will reproduce your faults!** Scary stuff!

But this is the way things happen in everyday life. If you are coaching someone to play a sport, you will coach them to play *the same way you do*. If you're teaching someone to play a musical instrument, you will consciously get them to *copy you*. An apprentice carpenter will learn their craft *by imitating the skills of the tradesperson they work with*. This doesn't mean that you will be *exactly the same* as the person who trains you, but you will certainly turn out to be *similar* to them.

The old saying: *"Don't do as I do, do as I say"* doesn't hold water. What a person *does* speaks far more powerfully than what they *say*. If you went to a weight-loss meeting, and your instructor was fat, then the chances of you losing

---

1. The Greek word "mathetes" is usually translated "disciple".

weight would be negligible *irrespective of how good their information was!*

"Like father, like son" is a better proverb for the discipling relationship. Any parent knows that they will grow their children to maturity by modelling adulthood to them. And the *father/son* relationship is a good biblical description of the discipling relationship. It is certainly a term that Paul uses to describe his relationship with Timothy.

You **will** reproduce what you are – for good or ill! So make sure that what you're imparting into a new disciple are things you really want them to learn!

2. It's a Bible-teaching relationship

Whatever you do in growing a young disciple, you must sow God's word into them. You want them to delight in God's word and to be fruitful as a result. Your aim for each disciple is the picture in Psalm 1:

> **Psalm 1:2-3** *"But his delight is in the law of the LORD, and on his law he meditates day and night. He is like a tree planted by streams of water, which yields its fruit in season and whose leaf does not wither. Whatever he does prospers."*

If you want your growing disciples to be *"like a tree planted by streams of water, being fruitful, and prospering,"* then they need to be constantly watered by God's word. You are the primary person who will do this for them.

Right at this point – depending on your gifts and passions – you are either frothing at the mouth with excitement, or shaking in your boots with fear! For those who love teaching the Bible, you don't need any encouragement at this point –

except perhaps to make sure your small group doesn't just turn into a *mini-sermon* from you every week! For those of you who are a little hesitant about your teaching gifts, you might just be a little nervous right now.

But whatever you're feeling, you need to know that you will be used by God to apply his word to the hearts of his disciples in a very significant way. If you're not primarily a Bible-teacher, you can still be a very good discipler. Perhaps you can plug into the Bible teaching at your church and discuss and apply the sermon in your discipleship group. Maybe you can use some very well prepared Bible study booklets, where other Bible teachers have done a lot of the work for you, and present it in a way that you can easily follow. You can even invite guests into your group to teach a particular emphasis from the Bible that you know you would struggle with if you had to do it by yourself. Wherever you are at, and whatever ministry gifts you have received from God, you will be influential in not just teaching God's word to your growing disciples, but helping them to apply it to their lives.

Ryan was a great leader on our youth ministry team. He was a whiz at administration and a key person in ministry "behind the scenes". He had a faithful heart and the attitude of a genuine servant. In his spiritual gifts analysis, his top ministry gift was "administration" closely followed by "helps".

He wanted to lead some Year 7 boys in a discipleship team. I was a little hesitant. I asked him about his Bible-teaching gifts. I asked him about his shepherding gifts. He admitted that these ranked a little low in his spiritual-gift mix, but he was determined to sow his heart into these boys. We made sure he had some good support in the Bible-teaching department, and we allowed him to head up this small team of growing disciples.

The result? He stayed with those boys for six years. He took them right through to the conclusion of High School. He poured his life into them, and shaped and modelled them as faithful disciples. His gifts of administration led to his group being one of the best organised of all our groups. His gift of helps led to this entire group developing servant hearts, and when they left school, almost the whole group became our resource leaders (our behind-the-scenes leaders) at Crossfire.

Was he primarily a Bible-teacher? No. Did he have to depend on pre-prepared Bible studies? Yes. Did he sow God's word into the hearts of these young men? Absolutely! Did he hold them accountable for living out God's word in their day-to-day lives? You bet! And God used his range of spiritual gifts and passions to enable him to achieve a wonderful result.

Teaching the Bible really matters because you want your growing disciples to understand that the guidelines for their life come from God – it is not just your wise thoughts and opinions. They need to know that the fundamentals for growing as God's person have been laid down by God himself and revealed to us in the pages of scripture. They need to grow in their understanding, so that they themselves can find out God's answers by going to the Bible, rather than always having to ask you what you think. And of course, you want to teach the Bible to them in such a way that they will be able to teach it to others!

3. It's a whole-of-life relationship

Somewhere along the line, some of us have reduced education to only what happens in a classroom. Do you want to learn something? Then sit in a classroom with a qualified teacher and you will learn. Now, there's nothing *wrong* with classroom learning. It's often a great environment to facilitate the exchange of information. **But it's not the only way to learn!** And in many cases – it's not the **best** way to learn.

Champion athletes are not produced by merely sitting them in a classroom. World-class musicians do not develop their skill by simply studying books. Leading doctors are not trained only by attending lectures. Carpenters, electricians, plumbers and all sorts of other tradespeople do not learn their craft by simply sitting at a desk.

Education is a whole-of-life experience. Far more is *caught* than *taught*. You learn how to do things by watching someone more skilled than you, then by copying, improving, and developing your own style. The *apprentice* model is sometimes under-valued in our world when it is compared with those studying at advanced tertiary levels who end up with a string of letters after their name. *But the apprentice model is the primary educational model that Jesus used to train his disciples.* And if you want to train disciples today, it is still the best model.

That means that your relationship with those whom you are discipling needs to be *whole-of-life*. If you want to help someone to grow as a disciple of Jesus, then you need to get involved in their life, and they need to get involved in your life. You need to share life experiences together so that both of you can learn and grow through them.

A growing disciple will learn far more about how to treat their family by watching the way *you* treat *your* family. By having them over at our house, they will learn how to be a loving husband or wife, a caring mum or dad, or a respectful and co-operative child. A growing disciple will learn far more about how a Christian deals with anger by watching you on the sporting field, or driving with you in traffic. A growing disciple will learn far more about witnessing to their friends by observing how *you* witness to *your* friends. Transforming a new believer into a world-changing disciple is not just a matter of finding the right textbook for them. It's about *training* them for a Christlike life by *demonstrating* for them a Christlike life.

If your plan to train disciples only consists of a weekly Bible class, then you will miss your mark. Nothing *wrong* with the weekly Bible class – indeed it might be *one factor* in your discipleship training plan, but living as a disciple of Jesus isn't something that you primarily learn in the classroom. You can't just have *"Discipleship 101"* and get a certificate at the end of a 10-week course. Jesus trained his disciples in the cut-and-thrust of daily life. We need to do the same.

As I reflect over the teenagers I have personally trained as disciples, it seems that the times I have been *most effective* is when I have taken this *whole of life* approach seriously, and allocated solid time to be involved in each disciple's life. And I seem to have been *least effective* when I haven't allocated this time, and have merely relied on our weekly Bible class to keep us going.

In a group setting, it's easy to assume that everyone's going okay. That everyone is on track with Jesus. That no-one is striking any difficulties. It's not until you spend some one-on-one time with a person that you pick up where they're struggling. Those individual catch-ups really make the difference. Having a milkshake after school; showing up to watch them at their sporting event; riding bikes together, fixing the car, trawling the shopping mall or working at a soup-kitchen. When the growing disciple gets to spend individual time with you, that's when they see what you're really like. And you get to see what *they're* really like.

4. It's a coaching relationship

At our youth ministry, we have weekly small groups to help train high-schoolers to be faithful disciples. We call these *"Discipleship Teams"* or *"D-Teams"*. Each small group has a leader, but we have intentionally called these leaders *"D-Team Coaches"*. The term *"coach"* captures the spirit of the relationship that a discipleship trainer has to his growing disciples. If you want to train disciples, then I urge you to think like a coach. How does a coach teach skills to their team? How do they mould them into a team to perform at their best? How do they develop each individual player so that all the coach has to do is to stand on the side-lines and encourage?

Here are the steps I learnt in my soccer coach's course:

i. Demonstrate the skill to the player. You do it – they watch.

ii. Do it with them. You both try it together.

iii. Get them to try it by themselves. They do it – you watch.

iv. Correct them where needed.

v. From your basic instruction, let them develop their own style.

vi. Stand on the sidelines and encourage like crazy!

As *discipleship coaches*, we will train our disciples the same way. How will you teach a new believer to have an individual time with God each day? You could try just telling them. (Some will pick this up and run with it.) You could have a Bible study about it and tell them to put it into action (Some may respond to this). But if we think of ourselves as coaches, our training might look something more like this:

i. Constantly refer to your own time with God – so they pick up it's an important part of a disciple's life. Then show them how you spend this time with God. You do it – they watch.

ii. Do it with them. You both try it together.

iii. Get them to try it by themselves. They do it – you watch.

iv. Correct them where needed.

v. Let them develop their own style.

vi. Stand on the sidelines and encourage like crazy!

If you adopt this *coaching* mentality, you will teach all aspects of discipleship in this manner. And I believe, you will then teach them far more effectively. Your aim as a coach is to teach and train them thoroughly, so that in the long term, they will stand strongly for Jesus *whether you are around or not.* You will train them to become more dependent on God, and less dependent on you.

5. It's a committed and intentional relationship

What's the difference between a discipling relationship,

and two Christians in the same Bible study who hang out a lot together? On the surface, you may not spot the difference. But there is a huge distinction between the two.

A discipling relationship is a *committed and intentional* relationship. It is a genuine friendship – it is authentic fellowship between Christian brothers or sisters – but it has a *specific intention*. There is an established goal to be reached. There are outcomes to be obtained. A commitment from both sides to achieve a result. Like a coach with an athlete, there is an agreed agenda. Within the context of genuine love, the relationship exists to help the new believer to be transformed into a world-changing disciple.

This will control everything you do. It will flavour the way you interact with God's word. It will influence the way you pray. It will guide the time that you spend together. You will both pour blood, sweat and tears into the relationship to achieve the following result – that both of you will be more faithful and more passionate about your ongoing growth as disciples. Yes, that's right – *both* of you. If you have entered into an effective discipling relationship, then the person being discipled, *and* the person training them as a disciple, should both be stronger as a result. *(More about this in a moment!)*

This intentional purpose *has* to be agreed on by both parties. It's a two-way commitment. If one member is a reluctant participator in the arrangement, then the discipling will not work. You might have the greatest passion to disciple another believer, but if they don't also have that passion and commitment to achieve the same result, then you *cannot* disciple a person who is not ready for it!

Some years ago, I was discipling half a dozen mid-teenage boys who had all been converted from non-Christian backgrounds. We used to meet as a discipleship group on Sunday afternoons, and then, after a bite to eat, we would all head off for church together.

I was red-hot keen to transform them into world-changing disciples. I thought (or maybe I just hoped!) that they shared the same passion. One Sunday afternoon, as we were studying the Bible together, I asked, *"Gary – can you please look up the Bible reference for Question 4?"* His reply? *"Why should I?"* I was stunned for a moment, and then retorted, *"Because it will help us all grow as disciples!"*

I thought this would settle the argument, but Gary had one more comment to make. *"I can't be bothered. Get Paul to look it up!"* I motioned to Paul that maybe that would be a good idea. *"Why should I do it?"* he asked. *"It's not my turn!"*

You see, there was a problem that I hadn't identified up to this point. I was fully committed to the goal of raising these boys as world-changing disciples, *but they weren't!* They were there for other reasons. They enjoyed the fellowship. They enjoyed having my undivided attention for an hour or two. They enjoyed the free food. They even enjoyed being Christians. *But they were not ready to be discipled!* So we stopped the discipling group, and we just hung out together for a while. We were still good friends – but we were no longer committed in that intentional way.

6. It's a two-way relationship

Throughout this book, I keep identifying the disciple who is being trained, and the disciple who is training them. My experience has been that this is the only way it works. *Someone* has to be the leader. In youth ministry, this is a fairly easy relationship to sort out. The adult is the trainer; the young person is the trainee. I acknowledge that when you're working with adults this distinction is a little harder to identify – especially if all participants are about the same age – but like a coach and an athlete, there needs to be a clear distinction about *which person takes the initiative to train the other.*

Having said all that, I want to make one thing clear – *this is not a one-way street!* If disciples are working and growing together, then irrespective of who is the trainer and who is the trainee, *both should be stronger in Christ as a result.* The biblical picture of the church is that no matter what our spiritual gifts, no matter what our experience, no matter what our role is – *we are in this together.*

In this sense the discipling relationship is deeper than a normal teacher/student or coach/athlete relationship. Can a student hold a teacher accountable for the amount of study hours the teacher is putting in? Can an athlete hold a coach accountable for the coach's individual fitness work? Probably not. But in a discipling relationship, the accountability is two-way. A discipleship trainer may well ask his trainee how they're going with their personal time with God, *but it is fully expected that the trainee can also ask the same question of their trainer!*

Some of the most joyous and fulfilling times in my walk as a Christian have been where those whom I was training as disciples have ministered back to me. They have loved me, cared for me, taught me, encouraged me, corrected me and rebuked me. Any discipleship trainer needs to be ready to submit themselves to the ministry of their trainee. No-one is above learning and growing. We're all in this together!

7. It's an accountable relationship

If there's one word that has revolutionised our discipleship teams that we have for our young people, it's this word – *accountability.* That is, we're not just there to learn information together – we're there to hold each other accountable for living out what we learn.

I can think back to a time before our discipling relationships had accountability as a key factor. On the surface, things didn't look much different. We met together in small groups. We studied the Bible. We answered the application questions. We prayed together, we fellowshipped together. Ask anyone as we finished up each week, and they could probably tell you something that they had learned. We had Bible studies about discipleship **but we weren't training disciples**. We were getting all the right information but there was no outcome that we were holding each other accountable to.

> Imagine you're having a Bible study about being generous. We discover from the Bible that God is a generous God, and that he wants his people to be generous like he is. There are some application questions where we try and put this into action in our own life. The question is raised about financial generosity to the work of God's church. We all agree that we need to be more generous with our giving.

We pray about it, head off home, and the following week we show up for the next topic in our Bible study. *(This is the way we used to operate!)*

Here's where accountability comes in: in addition to everything above, *we get specific* as to what *being generous with our giving* really means. We start talking hard figures. There are all sorts of encouragements going on to inspire us to be more generous. Before we finish we take a note of what each other has said, and we commit to pray for each other during the week on this specific issue.

The following week, when we show up for Bible study again, we start by asking: *"How did each person go with being more generous in their giving this week?"* Then there is a time of honest truth-telling. In an atmosphere of grace and forgiveness, we hold each other accountable for our obedience in this area. We encourage and spur each other on. If there has been a widespread difficulty on this issue *we do not go on to the next topic until we have worked it through.*

This is not done in a judgmental or condemning way. It is simply a band of brothers or sisters who hold each other accountable before their Father. And sometimes that accountability is the key factor that helps us to be more obedient to our God. Knowing that *no-one walks alone* can be a great encouragement!

I heard of a Christian businessman who had a particular struggle with pornography. He was about to go away on a business conference, and he knew from previous experience that the hotel where they were staying had in-house pornography channels available in every room.

All he would have to do was touch one button, and *no-one would ever know.*

How did he deal with this? He simply told his Christian brothers in his discipleship group that he was about to face this time of strong temptation. He asked them to pray for him, but also asked them to question him about it when he returned. The simple knowledge that he would have to answer to his fellow disciples gave him the strength to deal with the temptation and address it.

Accountability simply means *no-one walks alone.* That's the key to having *everyone* grow as disciples!

8. It's a long-term relationship

By now I'm sure you've worked out – this is no quick-fix relationship. Transforming a disciple isn't going to be achieved in a ten-week course. This is a long-term commitment to sow into people's lives in such a way that they are set on a course for life as a faithful disciple and a passionate disciple-maker. And because the relationship between the trainer and the trainee is paramount, you don't want your growing disciples to change leaders every year! You don't disciple people because your name's on the rota and it's *your turn.* You disciple them because you are committed to investing your life into theirs so that the kingdom of God grows.

Jesus took twelve men for three years. And even within this group, he was often just with "the three." I suspect that Jesus was a far better discipleship trainer than I am! He achieved results that seem far beyond my feeble efforts! In the past twenty tears, I have discipled three groups of young men. Most of them started at at age 11-14. I took each group for five or six years – and more or less saw them right through their high-school life. The people in each group changed a little from year to year, but basically for each group, it was more or less the same core people all the way through.

Not every leader in our youth ministry is able to take students all the way through high school, although many do. For each of my two children, they had three discipleship coaches during their six years of high school. But the aim is still the same – that when you sign up to transform new believers into world-changing disciples, you are committing yourself for a number of years.

Of course, it doesn't all stop once they are no longer in your group. I still have a very special place in my heart for all the young men whom I have been privileged to disciple over the years. I still pray for them – I am still in contact with many of them. Of course, many have moved to other parts of the world and have been planted into local churches, but to be honest, if any of them needed me, I would come running!

Okay – that's the kind of relationship you need to have if you're going to disciple anyone. But what sort of a person do you need to be if you're going to lead others? Read on!

Chapter 15

The faithful discipling leader

If you're going to train others to be disciples, what sort of leader do you need to be? And if you're going to train other disciples so that they too will be able to raise up yet more disciples, what sort of leaders do you need them to become?

1. Discipling by imitation

Here is the principle of *discipling by imitation* – "*who you are*" *is reproduced in those you lead.* In fact the key *method* of biblical discipleship is to have your growing disciples *deliberately imitate* what they see in their leader. Not that any of us will be perfect – but all of us are called to present a believable model that is able to be copied.

Here it is in a nutshell:

Question: *"How does a growing disciple know how to live as an obedient Christian?"*

Answer: *"By watching how their Christian leader deals with life, and modelling themselves on that."*

Sure – they will be modelled by God's word – they will be modelled by God's Spirit – but when push comes to shove, and a growing disciple is trying to work out *"What sort of a person am I meant to become?"* – they will look for a flesh-and-blood model so they have *someone to imitate*.

This principle of *discipling by imitation* is well embedded in the scriptures. Here's what Paul says to the growing disciples in Thessalonica:

> **2 Thessalonians 3:7, 9** *"For you yourselves know how you ought to follow our example … We did this … in order to make ourselves a model for you to follow."*

Paul continues this *discipling by imitation* as he helps to develop Timothy as a growing believer:

> **2 Timothy 1:13** *"What you heard from me, keep as the pattern of sound teaching."*

Paul summarises this same discipleship method when he writes to the Corinthians:

> **1 Corinthians 11:1** *"Follow my example, as I follow the example of Christ."*

There are many other passages in the Bible which commend this method of training disciples. [1] What does all this mean? **Who you are must match up to what you teach!** So if we investigate what the Bible says you are to *teach,* you can work out the *sort of teacher* that you're meant to be.

There are many passages in the Bible that give godly standards for Christian leaders. [2] But what I want to do here is take one chapter of Paul's instructions to Titus. By examining what Titus is instructed to *teach* to his growing disciples, we can work out by the principle of *discipling by imitation,* what sort of *leader* Titus needed to be so he would be effective.

---

1. See 1 Corinthians 4:16; Philippians 3:17, 4:9; 1 Thessalonians 1:6; Hebrews 6:12, 13:7; 2 Timothy 2:2.
2. The four key New Testament lists are 1 Timothy 3:1-7, 3:8-13; 2 Timothy 2:22-26 and Titus 1:5-9. These are analysed and discussed in detail in *Leaders Who Will Last* – Chapters 12 and 13.

So – what sort of person would make the best discipleship leader? And what sort of leadership should we train growing disciples to acquire?

2. Characteristics of a faithful leader – *from Titus 2*

a) A leader under God's authority

Titus Chapter 2 starts and finishes with similar commands:

> **Titus 2:1** *"You must teach what is in accord with sound doctrine."*

> **Titus 2:15** *"These, then, are the things you should teach. Encourage and rebuke with all authority."*

Titus is commanded to teach God's word in a way that is sound and authoritative. He is to stick to God's word – to make sure that what he teaches is in accord with established doctrine, and teach with the authority that God's word provides.

Paul gives Timothy similar instructions:

> **2 Timothy 2:15** *"Do your best to present yourself to God as one approved, a workman who does not need to be ashamed and who correctly handles the word of truth."*

So if Titus and Timothy, and anyone else who is going to train disciples are meant to teach God's word soundly, then *what sort of leaders do they need to be?* A person who lives soundly under God's authority! The principle of *discipling by imitation* demands that this must be true.

So if you're going to train others to be growing disciples,

you need to make sure that you yourself are modelling what it means to live soundly under God's authority. If you're organising other leaders to train various groups of disciples, then this is the first thing that you'll look for. Indeed, if you are raising up disciples – and training them to be future leaders, so that they too can raise up even more disciples – then you need to train them to be leaders who live soundly under God's authority.

> We have many small discipleship groups for our teenagers at our church. Maybe 40 or 50 in all. That means 40 or 50 youth leaders, each taking a handful of students and growing them into world-changing disciples. Some of these groups go brilliantly well. Others falter a little. But here is something that is almost always true in the groups that are faltering: *their leader has stopped living under God's authority in some area of their life.*

Do you want to be the ideal leader for growing young disciples? Then start by being a person who lives under God's authority.

b) A leader with a Christlike character

Titus is given a series of instructions as to how to apply God's word to different groups of disciples. He is given specific words for older men and older women, younger men and younger women. The exact instructions are different as they are applied to varying age groups. But see if you can pick out the pattern:

> **Titus 2:2** *"Teach the older men to be temperate, worthy of respect, self-controlled, and sound in faith, in love and in endurance."*

Titus 2:3 *"Likewise, teach the older women to be reverent in the way they live, not to be slanderers or addicted to much wine, but to teach what is good."*

Titus 2:4-5 *"Then they can train the younger women to love their husbands and children, to be self-controlled and pure, to be busy at home, to be kind, and to be subject to their husbands, so that no one will malign the word of God."*

Titus 2:6 *"Similarly, encourage the young men to be self-controlled."*

Every instruction is training these disciples to be *of Christlike character.* The point where they are most likely to stumble is highlighted. But following the principle of *discipling by imitation,* if you're going to teach others to have a Christlike character, *then you yourself need to be a leader with a Christlike character.*

So if you're looking for someone to be the trainer of disciples, here is another question to ask: *"Do I see in them a growing Christlike character?"* If you're raising up disciples to become leaders in their own right, then you need to ask the same question.

When I started training disciples, I was very *gung-ho* about the whole deal. Meticulously organised; painstakingly methodical; precise and intentional. We had the right curriculum; we had the right discipline; we had the right vision. And God worked through all this! But if you asked the question: *"Did I display a growing Christlike character?"* the truthful answer probably was *"Not very obviously".* I had all the passion to achieve great things in ministry, but none of the relational Christlikeness that was worth imitating. People were prepared to work with me because they liked the direction of the ministry – but I'm not sure that anyone *wanted* to work with me!

Do you want to be a great discipling leader? Do you want to raise others to be great discipling leaders? Then focus on growing a *Christlike character* that can be imitated and reproduced. Otherwise you will build a red-hot ministry that may collapse one day like a house of cards.

c) A leader who sets the example

All of this is summarised well in the next verse:

> **Titus 2:7** *"In everything set them an example by doing what is good."*

This is the principle of *discipling by imitation* at work. Do you want to develop disciples with any particular strengths or attitudes? Then model those strengths and attitudes yourself.

d) A leader of integrity

> **Titus 2:7-8** *"In your teaching show integrity, seriousness and soundness of speech that cannot be condemned, so that those who oppose you may be ashamed because they have nothing bad to say about us."*

If there's one key word that summarises the heart of a great discipleship leader, it is this one: *integrity*. All that means is: *what you see is what you get*. No pretence. The outside matches the inside. The image matches the substance. There are no hidden secrets. You are genuine *the whole way through*.

Because, by following the principle of *discipling by imitation*, producing disciples of integrity demands we have leaders of integrity. Then these disciples of integrity whom we produce will become the future leaders of integrity. If this is the standard that we maintain in our ministry, then no-one will be able to condemn us! Sometimes those who take short-cuts might *appear* to get ahead. But in the long-term *integrity always wins,* because it is God's way, and all his ways are good and right.

e) A leader who submits

There is a specific word given to slaves who had become Christians:

> **Titus 2:9** *"Teach slaves to be subject to their masters in everything, to try to please them, not to talk back to them."*

Paul is teaching Titus the importance of submission to authority. Here he does not debate the pros and cons of a system that depends on slaves – he simply addresses those slaves who were legally bound to their masters. The attitude of a genuine disciple is that they will joyfully submit to rightful authority.

The principle of submission is well-entrenched in scripture:

> **Ephesians 5:21** *"Submit to one another out of reverence for Christ."*

There are many situations where disciples are specifically called on to display this submission as evidence of their Christlike character. Children are to submit to parents; slaves are to submit to masters; and we could add a host of modern-day equivalents.

Here is the key to being a great discipleship leader: *if you need to **teach** submission as a normal part of Christian life, then you need to **model** submission in your own life first.*

Do you want to be a great discipleship leader? Then joyfully submit to those in authority over you. Do you want to train disciples to be great leaders? Then model submission to them, and teach them to imitate.

> I was in a church once where I did not see eye-to-eye with the senior pastor. I thought he was wrong on a number of issues. Even though I was meant to be ministering under his vision, I let it be known where I opposed him. That's how I led my discipleship group – and that's how I let them down. *I did not model submission to them – so they did not learn to be submissive.* I would say things like: *"Well, the church has said we really shouldn't do things this way, **but we're going to do it anyway!**"*
>
> There was nothing Christlike about my attitude, and I reproduced that rebellious attitude in those whom I discipled. And guess who they ended up being unsubmissive to? Me! I had taught them well! The principle of *discipling by imitation* came back to bite me!

You will not get far if you have unsubmissive leaders on your team. They will reproduce this in their growing disciples, which will result in a whole new unsubmissive generation. So check it out – are there areas where you might be reproducing an unsubmissive attitude in those whom you lead?

f) A leader who can be trusted

Titus 2:10 *"show that they can be fully trusted, so that in every way they will make the teaching about God our Saviour attractive."*

This is the conclusion of God's word to the slaves. As well as being submissive, they also need to be trustworthy. If this is what Titus is meant to teach, then, following the principle of *discipling by imitation* before leaders can teach *about* trustworthiness, they need to be leaders who *are* trustworthy.

When you plan to meet up with a disciple – by themselves or in a group – can you be trusted to be there, on time? When personal information is shared within your group, can you be trusted to keep it confidential? When you say you will do something, do you do it? When you say to *God* you will do something, do you do it?

If you are not trustworthy as a leader, then no-one will trust you. And if no-one trusts you, then no-one will follow you. People will only follow a leader whom they trust. If you want others to follow you, then you must model and live a life of trust. If you want to raise up disciples to be leaders of others, then you just teach them to do the same.

g) A leader who responds to God's grace

God's grace is absolutely fantastic! God does something for me that I do not deserve. God reaches out to me with love and forgiveness and accepts me despite my sin and my rebellion. This is great stuff – as the next verse says:

Titus 2:11 *"For the grace of God that brings salvation has appeared to all men."*

Here's the problem with how we often respond to God's grace: *because we know he'll forgive us, we don't bother about obeying him that much!*

So, what response to God's grace do we want from a leader who will influence and train many other disciples?

> **Titus 2:11-12** *"For the grace of God that brings salvation has appeared to all men. It teaches us to say "No" to ungodliness and worldly passions, and to live self-controlled, upright and godly lives in this present age."*

We need leaders who will say "no" to ungodliness so that they might produce a whole new generation of disciples who will also say "no" to ungodliness. Does that describe you? Does that describe the disciples whom you are growing? Does that describe the leaders whom you are raising? The leaders that God wants – the hearts that he wants reproduced in others – are those who respond to his grace by saying "no" to ungodliness.

h) A leader centred around Jesus

Deep down, this is the sort of leader that we need to train the next generation of disciples: one whose whole life revolves around Jesus and what he has done for us. Check out the next verses:

> **Titus 2:13-14** *"while we wait for the blessed hope — the glorious appearing of our great God and Saviour, Jesus Christ, who gave himself for us to redeem us from all wickedness and to purify for himself a people that are his very own, eager to do what is good."*

We need leaders who have been purified by Jesus' death

and resurrection, who are eager to do good as they wait in hope of the Lord's great return. This is so important to remember in a discipleship programme. In the end it's not our ministry strategy that will make it work; it is not our well-organised network of small groups; it is not our super-slick curriculum; nor our high standards and challenges. The thing that will make disciples of Jesus – *lasting* disciples who will go out and change the world for him – is to raise up people who are actually *disciples of Jesus.* Centred on him. Controlled by him. Living for his death. And dying for his life. And if that's the quality of disciples that God wants us to raise up, then guess what sort of leaders we need to be? We must be *Jesus-centred* leaders who:

> **2 Corinthians 4:10** *"always carry around in our body the death of Jesus, so that the life of Jesus may also be revealed in our body."*

There are many helpful characteristics for those who will lead other disciples. But the key qualities are determined by the principle of *discipling by imitation*. This simply means that anything we want to teach a growing disciple – *we have to be living it first.*

When you're working out whether you are ready to train other disciples, ask these questions: "*Am I happy for these disciples to live their Christian lives just as I do? Do I have a heart for Jesus that is worth reproducing in them? Am I living a Christian life that in all conscience I am happy for them to imitate?*" No-one gets it right all the time. Our model will always be imperfect. But with your ups and downs, with your pluses and minuses, with your strengths and weaknesses, with your victories and struggles – are you happy to be the imperfect model that others will imitate?

Do you want to select leaders who would be ideal to train other disciples in your church? Then ask the same questions. Do you want to raise up disciples so that *they* will be great leaders of disciples in the future? Then raise them the same way. Model Christlikeness for them; model repentance for them; and then the words that you teach them will have the credibility of your changed life.

Who are your most effective discipleship leaders? Answer: your most Christlike leaders – your most faithful leaders. Always.

Chapter 16
The effective discipling leader

1. Being both faithful and effective

To transform new believers into world-changing disciples, we need to have leaders with two overall qualities: – they need to be *faithful;* they also need to be *effective.* Being *faithful* has to do with being Christlike – being biblical – displaying all the qualities outlined in the previous chapter. Being *effective* simply means having the wisdom to put these faithful characteristics to work in a way that achieves the best possible outcome. The two must work together. You can't be effective without first being faithful. *But you can be faithful without being effective!*

Imagine that God has laid on your heart a vision for making disciples at the local state high school. You feel compelled by God to proclaim his word at this location, to call students to follow Jesus and to equip them to change the world for him. *(Excellent vision! Very close to my heart!)*

Being *faithful* means you obey God. You live a life that is worthy of a follower of Jesus. You obey God's call and prayerfully start ministering at your local high school. You start sharing God's word and calling on students to respond. That's all about being *faithful.*

Being *effective* answers the next question: *What methods will you use to most effectively call students to respond?*

- *Do you fly a helicopter over the school and preach to them through a megaphone?*
- *Do you stand in the corner of the school yard as a street preacher?*
- *Do you help the school out as a tutor or a coach and build relationships with individual students?*
- *Do you run a large lunchtime outreach group?*
- *Do you start a before-school Bible study?*
- *Do you visit staff-rooms to build relationships with the teachers?*

These are not essentially *biblical* questions; they are *wisdom* questions. Whether or not you are successful in making disciples at that high school won't just depend on whether you are *faithful* – it will also depend on how *effective* you are.

We have already looked at some of the characteristics of a *faithful* discipling leader. Let's now check out what it means to be an *effective* discipling leader. The *faithful* characteristics come from the Bible. The *effective* characteristics come from wisdom based on experience.

2. Characteristics of an effective leader

a) You are available

Discipling others is a big commitment. It is not a short sprint – it is a long-distance event. Before you begin the journey with your fellow-disciples, you need to check out whether you are able to last the distance. Here are some factors to consider:

- *Can I make this my "Number One Ministry" for the next 2-3 years?*

- *Am I prepared to leave aside other ministries to make way for this?*
- *Do I need to cut back on other interests and distractions to be an effective discipler?*
- *How will this affect my family relationships? Am I able to sow into other disciples without sacrificing my time with my own family?* **Do I have the support of my family?**
- *Am I prepared for those unexpected moments when someone I am discipling really needs me in a crisis?*

b) You are discerning

When you are discipling others, you need to know when to tackle issues head-on, and when to roll with the punches. You need to be able to discern which are the issues that must be addressed straight away, and which are the situations that might not be ideal, but it's okay to leave them to another day.

I was meeting with my discipleship group of Year 9 boys. We had been together for about two years, and were making a moderate amount of progress in growing as Jesus' disciples.

I asked the boys what they would like to do in their future. In the middle of discussions about being business people, performing artists, medical missionaries and multi-millionaires, Oliver suddenly came out with a statement that stopped everyone in their tracks:

"I want to become a Buddhist monk!"

On the spur of the moment, I had to discern whether this was a "crisis of faith" issue, or a mild distraction in the turbulent life of a pubescent teenager.

"A Buddhist monk?" I replied. *"Why would you want to become a Buddhist Monk?"*

"Because I want to experience the peace that they have."

"Okay. I can understand that." (I think I was *struggling* to understand it, but I wanted Oliver to know that I was working hard at listening!) I thought I should probe a little further. *"Do you believe what the Buddhists would say about God?"*

"No way – what they believe is a pile of garbage!"

"So let me understand this. You don't think they have the truth about God, but you'd like to experience the peace that they have?"

At this point, I didn't see the need to do a complete analysis of the Christian faith as opposed to the Buddhist faith. It wasn't time to launch an attack on world religions. I simply had a Year 9 boy, struggling to be faithful to Jesus, who was not experiencing peace in his life. It seemed to me this was a pastoral issue, not a theological issue. It was something for us to chat about the next time we caught up one-on-one.

Was I right in my discernment? Only time will tell. But to be an effective discipling leader, you need to learn when it is right to tackle issues head-on, and when it is wiser to wait for another day.

c) You are organised

Some people are *super-organised* – others are much more *spur of the moment*. There's not one single model that we all need to live up to, and it's okay to be genuinely yourself in the way that you do things. But if you're going to be effective at training disciples, you need to develop a reasonable level of organisation *whether it comes naturally to you or not.*

You will discover that if you aren't reasonably organised in the way you train other disciples, you will have a hard time getting others to follow your lead. Disorganisation leads to disillusionment. No-one is motivated to perform better if the person responsible for them is totally disorganised.

If you want to inspire those you are discipling, here are some key areas to maintain a high standard of organisation:

- *There needs to be a written plan of the dates, times and locations of where you meet. Something that can be stuck on the front of the fridge. Something that each disciple can check with. Something that parents can refer to!*

- *You need to plan ahead so that Bible-study books are ordered well in advance and are ready for everyone when it's time to start. I have discovered the principle of the Urgency/Stock Ratio is well entrenched. Translated, this simply means: the more urgent your need to buy Bible-study books, the more likely that the bookstore will be out of stock! Don't leave it to the last minute!*

- *If you want to start your group on time, then you need to be there first! Even if you need to pick people up on the way, be organised enough so that you are the first to arrive. I like to arrive at least 15 minutes before a group starts. This sort of organisation inspires confidence in the other group members.*

> • *If you're catching up with disciples individually, you need to keep track of who you saw – and when. Otherwise you mightn't remember who you have seen – and who you haven't. Or you may not realise how long it is since you've caught up with a particular individual. It is very easy to accidentally leave someone out. And even if you don't notice, I can guarantee that they will!*

d) You are adaptable

If you are a well-organised person, here is an important lesson you need to learn: you need to be prepared to change your well-engineered plans at the last minute! Because the world is sometimes chaotic, and because people are individuals and sometimes react very differently to each other, you need to be flexible and adaptable in your approach.

I led a group of middle-high-school boys once. I had my carefully prepared discipleship studies and I was following a tried-and-true formula that had worked well with every other discipleship group I had led. But these boys were different. The high point of our group time wasn't when we were discovering amazing truths from the Bible or being challenged in an area of obedience. The group came to life when they started *debating* things with each other. They liked to test theories and explore them. They wouldn't settle for my succinct and pithy answers. They wanted to argue things through – and push all theories to preposterous lengths.

I sort of twigged this when they were in Year 8. I was simply trying to teach them that we need to be faithful managers of our time – and I discovered that they had initiated a debate as to whether time was *linear* or *circular!* And they were passionate about the argument! I couldn't even understand why it mattered! *(Still don't!)*

Here's where I had to be adaptable: I soon discovered that my *favoured method of teaching didn't match their favoured method of learning.* I had to change my carefully thought-through plans simply because I had a very different bunch of individuals.

So be prepared to be adaptable and flexible. You might discover that what motivates most of your students does not work for one particular individual – and you may need to change for the sake of that person. You might find that the issue which *you* think is the most important one to tackle has been overshadowed by another issue which is more current for your disciples. You might arrive for your group with your hour and a half all carefully timetabled – and discover in the first 60 seconds that one of your group members is in tears because of something which just happened at home.

Be organised. But be adaptable.

e) You have a sense of humour

Some people are really funny – others struggle to get the punch-line right for the simplest of jokes. You don't need to be funny to train disciples, but you do need to have a sense of humour. Sometimes you just need to collapse in laughter. Sometimes you need to learn not to take yourself so seriously.

I was in a small group where one of the boys, called

Mick, was about to enter the Navy. He was in his late teens, and this was the last time he was going to be present in our discipling group. We were having a time of prayer, and I know that some of the other boys were concerned that the Navy would be a difficult place to be a Christian, and they wanted to pray for Mick's protection.

In a group prayer-time, Brett was praying for his best friend Mick who was about to sail the seven seas. It was a quiet and intimate moment. Brett's prayer went something like this:

*"Lord I pray for Mick in this new chapter of his life. I pray that you will keep him strong as a Christian and that as he joins the Navy, he won't **drift away**".*

It was a sincere prayer in a very tender and quiet moment. But as soon as the words *"drift away"* were heard, you could hear other group members starting to laugh. It commenced as a small snigger, but it started to grow. I opened my eyes and noticed that the boys were laughing and smiling at each other, and the small snicker was developing into full-blown belly laughs. Very soon, everyone was joining in – repeating the words *"drift away"* and enjoying the irony of these unwitting comments.

What's a discipleship leader to do at this point? Sternly remind people that they are in the presence of God and not to take him lightly? Castigate group-members for daring to laugh? I simply joined in the fun! Our emotions were all heightened because Mick was leaving us, and the laughter was a welcome release. We all laughed together, we all enjoyed the moment, and when it had died down, we resumed praying and praising God that we could enjoy being together in his presence.

A sense of humour. I don't understand how anyone could work with young people and survive without one. I don't understand how anyone could effectively disciple new believers without having a hearty laugh with them from time to time.

The work we are doing – of transforming new believers into world-changing disciples – is serious work. But lighten up! Don't take *yourself* too seriously!

f) You are a listener

Sometimes I am so keen to teach others that I forget to listen. If you want to be a great leader, you need to be a great listener. Not just listening to the words that the other person is saying *(although that's not a bad start!)* but also listening to *what they might mean, how they might be feeling,* and *what's **not** being said.*

> Aaron was a teenager in our youth group. A little on the spiritual fringe – but always there – always joining in. We didn't see him once he left school. Ten years later, he showed up at church as a young man in his late twenties. I recognised him – and chatted briefly with him after church.
>
> I admit, I was rather busy. I was about to go away on two weeks' vacation. I had a stack of people to see and a load of loose ends to attend to before I could get away. That evening at church, all I had on my mind was that I would probably be up after midnight trying to get everything done, and the *last* thing I needed was to put anything extra on the pile.

When Aaron caught up with me, we reminisced for a moment about the good old days at our youth group, and then he asked, *"Can we catch up for coffee sometime?"*

"Absolutely" I replied. *"I'm going away for two weeks, but as soon as I'm back, let's catch up!"*

"No problems," he muttered. *"I'll see you then."* We finished our conversation and both moved on to other things.

About half an hour later, one of our associate pastors chatted with me. *"Did that young man who was looking for you find you?"* he asked. *"That young man whose child has just been killed?"*

I stopped suddenly with my eyes transfixed like a rabbit caught in the headlights. *"His child has just been killed?"*

"Yes – he wanted to talk to you about it. Did you catch up with him?"

Oh my goodness! I prayed fast – I ran fast – I caught up with him in the car-park. Then I started doing the one thing that I had been too busy to do earlier on – *I started listening to him.* We talked together, we cried together, we walked together. I had almost abandoned a person in real need because I was too busy to listen.

Sometimes I am so full of my own answers that I don't make the time to listen to the other person's questions. If you want to be a great discipling leader, you need to learn to be a great listener. The disciples you are training are not robots to be programmed; they are real human beings with real needs and real feelings. If you fail to listen, you fail to disciple.

g) You are a questioner

I love it when growing disciples ask me questions – because so often I think I know the answer! And there's something within me that *loves* being right *(happens from time to time!)*. But here is something I learned in my very early days of discipling: *if I simply give an answer, I am robbing the questioner of the joy of discovery.* I might feel powerful and superior because I have provided an excellent answer, but I have not empowered the growing disciple to learn how to discover things for themselves. If I merely give correct answers to probing questions, I am making the growing disciple more dependent on me and less able to fend for themselves.

When a growing disciple asks you a question, rather than *giving* them an answer, can you think of a question that will help them discover the answer for themselves? Because, if they can discover the answer for themselves, while it might take a whole lot longer, *they will **own** their answer far more strongly, and will be better equipped to work out their own solutions next time.*

Gary was in Year 12 and a member of my discipleship group. During Bible study, he asked me: *"If I'm going to honour Jesus in my relationship with my girlfriend, physically how far can I go with her?"*

I managed to resist the temptation to say: *"The Bible says a, b, c and d"*, and I simply replied with: *"Well, what do you think the Bible says?"* As he answered, I was able to help him clarify his position with further questions. *"What makes you say that? If that is true, what do you make of this verse? How might your idea play out in this scenario?"* The further we went, the more he discovered biblical truth for himself. *Eventually,* he came up with an answer which was something like what I would have said to him up front. But because *he* had done the work, it was *his* answer and he was now prepared to own it himself and live by it.

Learn to ask questions. Questions that will help your growing disciples to experience the joy of discovery. Questions that will help growing disciples become more dependent on God, and less dependent on you. Questions that will open their minds to the truths God wants to reveal to them. Questions that will help transform new believers into world-changing disciples.

The missing links of discipling

SECTION 5

In these last four chapters, I have listed what I believe are so often the four "missing links" of discipling. These are four key elements that often get missed out as we tackle the issue of transforming new believers into world-changing disciples.

I have seen many discipleship models in operation – and over the decades I have worked hard at getting discipleship ministries up and running.

I present to you the following four elements that I believe often get missed out or under-done.

1. The importance of keeping track

We had a guest speaker visit our youth ministry once. It was an evangelistic night where we were going to ask students to make decisions to follow Jesus. This was going to be the beginning of their discipleship adventure. The visiting speaker assured me that he felt confident in explaining the gospel and inviting students to respond.

It was a good message. It was a good invitation. But at the time of asking students to respond, he said: *"I want everyone in the auditorium to bow their heads and close their eyes."* I kept my eyes open at that stage. I guess I wanted to see what would happen. Then the speaker added *"I want **everyone** to bow their heads and close their eyes – that includes leaders!"* We then dutifully followed his instructions.

He continued: *"With every head bowed and with every eye closed, I want you to put your hand in the air if you want to say 'yes' to Jesus for the first time. Thank you – I see that hand. Thank you – there's another. Keep those eyes closed – keep those hands up – thank you – I see more hands going up – thank you."*

He then prayed for everyone who had raised their hand – assured them that they had started the most exciting journey of their life – and told them to put their hands down and for everyone else to open their eyes. We finished the night with a bang, and everyone agreed it had been a great success.

"Eight of your students became Christians tonight!" he said excitedly as I met him at the side of the stage.

"Great!" I replied. *"Who were they?"*

"Oh – I dunno. There was a blonde-haired kid near the back – there was a girl with a black top on – no, wait there – it might have been a dark blue top – oh I dunno – I don't know your students that well! But wasn't it great that eight of them responded?"

My reply? *"But if we don't know who they are, how can we turn them into lasting disciples?"*

That night we decided that the next time we did anything like that, we would work hard at keeping track of those who made decisions for Christ, and that we would work hard at keeping track of their growth as disciples every step of the way. *"If we don't know who they are, how can we turn them into lasting disciples?"*

If you belong to a very small church with a very small youth group, and you only see one new student become a Christian every year or so, then you won't have this problem. It will all be very personal and everyone will know how everyone is going. But as soon as you have more than one new disciple at a time, you need a way to track their progress so that none of them gets lost along the way.

My observation of churches who do not track the progress of their disciples? Their disciples do not usually hang in there for the long haul. They do not last. They simply slip through the cracks.

2. Tracking the initial response

Whenever anyone becomes a Christian, you need to be able to enter their details *right there and then*. Whether they come to Christ through the witness of an individual Christian, or through an organised event, you need to have a system where it is easy to enter their details and keep track of their growth.

In our youth ministry, we have always used a *Response Form*. Something that can easily be filled in whenever a student makes a commitment to Jesus. [1] It doesn't need to be complicated, but I would suggest it contain space for the following information:

- *Name and contact details of the student concerned.*
- *Enough details to classify age-group of person responding (we ask for school attended and year at school).*
- *Date and event where they responded.*
- *Name and contact details of the person who helped them respond.*
- **Clarification of what their response was.** *We have used the following categories:*
    - *First-time commitment*
    - *Wants to become a Christian, but hasn't done it yet*
    - *Re-commitment*
    - *Just asking questions*
    - *Just supporting a friend*

Once these forms have been filled in, the real fun begins!

---

1. A sample of our Response Form can be found in Appendix 4.

3. Follow-up needs an administrative component

If you have more than one person becoming a Christian at the same time, then you need an administrative process to keep track of them. If you can't be faithful in following-up two new believers, then don't pray for God to send you twenty new believers!

Shortly after people make a decision to follow Jesus, their details need to be entered in a database. The same is true if your students attend a ministry event organised by another Christian group. If you receive notification that they have made a response to Jesus, they too need to go on the database so that they can be tracked.

4. Follow-up is not only administration

While an administration system is needed to keep track of a number of new believers, never lose sight of the fact that a discipling ministry is not *primarily* an administrative one. It is a pastoral ministry. We are dealing with real people with real needs and real eternities.

We want to have the same vision as Jesus:

> **John 6:39** *"And this is the will of him who sent me, that I shall lose none of all that he has given me, but raise them up at the last day."*

The reason that we put high priority on tracking the discipleship of new believers is that *we don't want to lose any!* If any new believers do end up giving up, we want to make sure that it wasn't because of our sloppy follow-up! To keep Jesus' vision before us, we have John 6:39 written out in full across all our database printouts of new believers.

5. Follow-up needs constant tracking

If you have had an evangelistic event where twenty students have made first-time commitments to Jesus, how do you track them?

Here are the things that should already have happened in the first week: [2]

- *There has been an initial conversation at the moment they responded to Jesus.*
- *They have received a follow-up phone call.*
- *They have had a face-to-face catch-up.*
- *They have received a welcoming letter.*
- *They have been brought to a church event.*
- *They have been brought to a specific discipling ministry.*

Here's how you track this: *this information needs to be fed back into the original database.* And here's why: *as you meet each week as a team of leaders, you will review the follow-up database to check how things are going with each person.*

You need to be able to spot whether any of the steps above has not been completed for any reason. That is, has a particular student who responded received their initial phone call? Or their initial face-to-face contact? *If for any reason any of these steps has not been completed, you can take immediate action to rectify the problem.* But this needs to happen in the first week. No use finding out a month or so later that the person who was meant to follow them up got sick and never did it!

---

2. See more detail in Chapter 9.

6. Track each disciple until follow-up is concluded.

How long does a person who has responded remain on the initial follow-up database? *Until their follow-up reaches a logical conclusion.* Now I am using that word *conclusion* carefully – because, in one sense, no-one's discipleship is ever concluded. But here's what I mean: the new disciple stays on the initial follow-up database until one of two things have happened:

- *They have been firmly planted in an ongoing discipleship group (and under the care of their own discipler).*

- *Or, despite our best efforts, they have indicated that they no longer want to continue as a disciple.*

But until one of these two conclusions is reached, they remain on that initial follow-up database and they are reviewed every week to try and help them reach the next step in their discipleship. My experience has been that unless this is done meticulously – week in, week out – there is a high chance that those who made an initial response will not follow through to reach maturity in Christ.

If, of course, any person who has responded does decide to pull out and not continue, it doesn't mean that you no longer care for them! There may well be other ministries at your church that you can invite them to – to help them once again make a commitment that will last. But take them off the follow-up database, so you are only reviewing people who want to continue.

And if a disciple is growing well, and they are planted in an ongoing discipleship group, their progress still needs to be tracked. There may well be other ministries that your church would want to offer them. You need to know when they have been trained as leaders. You need to know when they are ready to start training other disciples. So, in one sense, the tracking never stops. But they no longer need to be on the initial follow-up database.

I have found that one of the missing links in effective discipleship is keeping track of new believers in those first few weeks and months. I urge you to take this component of administration seriously!

Chapter 18

Getting disciples into active ministry

I have observed a variety of discipleship programmes. Many of them have been used by God to grow new believers in amazing ways. But if there is sometimes a missing link that stops the process reaching its most effective conclusion, it's this one: *the discipleship programme is theoretical and never gets the new believer into active ministry.*

Strange, isn't it? The whole purpose of training up another disciple is so that they will be transformed into a world-changing disciple. The way we know that we are doing our job is when we see disciples unleashed in this world, and starting to reproduce in others the life-change that has already happened in them. That's the whole point of being a disciple! That's the only mission that Jesus left for us!

And yet it is so easy to end up thinking that the whole point of getting someone into a discipleship programme – *is to get them into the discipleship programme!* I have been at places where they're happy if they have most of their Christians meeting in small home groups. *(This is a good thing!)* But if those home groups are not raising up disciples who are going out and winning others to Jesus – then the home group might be serving no kingdom purpose at all.

So – one of the *missing links* in transforming new believers into world changing disciples is this: *get them into active ministry from the word go!*

1. How Jesus called his first disciples

Can we check back how Jesus called his first disciples to follow him? This is how Mark records it – right at the beginning of Jesus' ministry:

> **Mark 1:16-17** *"As Jesus walked beside the Sea of Galilee, he saw Simon and his brother Andrew casting a net into the lake, for they were fishermen."Come, follow me," Jesus said..."*

This is where Jesus calls Simon and Andrew to follow him. They are among Jesus' very first disciples. Now think for a moment: If you were Jesus, what motivation would you give people for following you? If you had to give them one compelling reason as to why they should follow you, what would you say to them? If you were Jesus, and you walked up to two fishermen, and you said to them: *"Come, follow me... and..."* – how would you finish the sentence?

> *"Come, follow me and ... I'll give you eternal life? ... I'll take you to heaven? ... I'll forgive all your sins?"*

All these are true, but that's not what Jesus said. In fact he doesn't say *"Come follow me and I will do **anything** for you."* You know what he said!

> **Mark 1:17** *"'Come, follow me,' Jesus said, 'and I will make you fishers of men'."*

Jesus says: *"When you join my kingdom – when you follow me – when you give up your life and trust everything into my hands – here's what I want you to do. I have a job for you. I want to put you on my ministry team. I will equip you to go and make more disciples."* What Jesus is saying very plainly is: *"When you become a disciple, you also become a disciple-maker".*

That is the very first thing that Jesus teaches his new disciples. In the same sentence that he first calls them to follow him, he teaches them about also bringing their friends to follow him as well. This is Jesus' first instruction on how to be a disciple. This is *"Discipleship 101"*. When Jesus calls anyone to be a disciple, he also calls them to be a disciple-maker.

2. The ministry team in action

In the very next chapter, look at what happens the moment that Levi responds to Jesus' call to become a disciple:

> **Mark 2:14-15** *"As he walked along, he saw Levi son of Alphaeus sitting at the tax collector's booth. 'Follow me,' Jesus told him, and Levi got up and followed him. While Jesus was having dinner at Levi's house, many tax collectors and 'sinners' were eating with him and his disciples, for there were many who followed him."*

It looks as if Levi has put into action his master's command to become a *"fisher of men"*. It seems as though the first thing he did after he became a disciple was to invite his tax-collector mates to a party – and he invited Jesus as well. I suspect that he probably then sat back and watched the spiritual fireworks! I don't know exactly what spiritual gifts Levi had, or whether he had any training for ministry, but I suspect that there are probably tax-collectors in heaven now because Levi learnt the first lesson of discipleship – *that when Jesus calls you to be a disciple, he also calls you to be a disciple-maker!*

Just four chapters later, we see the whole team in action as they minister to others.

> **Mark 6:6-13** *"Then Jesus went round teaching from village to village. Calling the Twelve to him, he sent them out two by two and gave them authority over evil spirits. ... They went out and preached that people should repent. They drove out many demons and anointed many sick people with oil and healed them."*

That's the way Jesus trained his disciples. He got them into front-line ministry. And I suspect that's still the way he wants us to train disciples today.

So how do we do that? Here are some keys that I've found really helpful over the past few decades:

3. Get new believers into frontline ministries

Sometimes when we think about getting new believers into ministry, we can be thinking of getting them to do usher duty or car-park duty at church; or getting them onto the church cleaning team; or into the band or drama group. There is nothing wrong with all these ministries. And new believers will take their place on these teams in due course. But the *key* ministries to get a new believer into are the absolute *frontline* ministries – those where they seek to reach out to others and try and help them to follow Jesus as well. No training course; no diploma; no Bible college. One of the keys to effective discipling is to get new believers into *frontline* ministries.

4. Get them witnessing from the word go

One of the keys to raising up a disciple who will be active in winning others to Jesus for the rest of their life is to start them in this frontline ministry *immediately* after they become a Christian. Not in Week 10; not after they have done a church training course; not after their first few discipleship meetings – but *straight away.*

Right from the word go. As soon as someone has made a commitment to follow Jesus, let them know that Jesus has a job for them to do. They need to help other people discover Jesus as well. And it can be as simple as inviting a non-Christian friend to come to your church service or youth group – or any other Christian event. When you make this a focus of those *first steps* that you take a new believer through, you will discover the amazing principle – *"New people bring new people"*. Often your *best* witnessing ministries will come through the contacts of those who have only recently been saved. They usually have good contacts in the non-christian world and they are often excited to share the life-changing news of Jesus with them.

5. Get them praying for their unsaved friends

In addition to getting new believers active in witnessing from the word go, you will want to give them some strategy and some training. A very simple way to do this is to instruct them on how to pray for three unsaved friends – and then to look for opportunities to win them to Christ.

Once again this needs to be right at the beginning of the journey. In our *Discipleship Training* Series, Week 2 introduces the idea of being a disciple-maker, and Week 3 teaches new believers how to pray for their unsaved friends. It is a simple thing that every Christian can do – it is a ministry that can have a profound effect – and yet it is a ministry that is easily neglected. Pray for each other's unsaved friends when you meet in your discipleship group; encourage each other to look for opportunities to win them to Christ, and invite them to Christian events – let the new believer know that their ministry of prayer will be powerful in changing other people's lives.

6. Get them telling their story

Everyone who has had their life changed by Jesus has a story to tell. They might not know that much about Jesus – they might not have figured out every facet of the Christian life – they might not be able to answer every question that comes their way – but there is one thing they can testify to: Jesus has changed their life!

There's an interesting encounter in *Mark 5,* where Jesus completely changes the life of a man who has been possessed by demons. A miraculous transformation! You can imagine that this man would want to spend the rest of his days with Jesus – to never leave his side but to know that he was right next to him, able to deal with any problem that came his way.

There is a fascinating exchange between Jesus and this transformed man as Jesus is trying to leave the region in a boat:

> **Mark 5:18** *"As Jesus was getting into the boat, the man who had been demon-possessed begged to go with him."*

You can imagine the scene. Jesus means so much to this man that he never wants to leave him. And yet Jesus is about to sail away from the area. So the transformed man begs Jesus to take him with him. There is safety in Jesus.

There is security in Jesus. There is comfort in Jesus.

But that's not where Jesus wants his new disciples! Yes – he wants our lifelong commitment! Yes – he has promised to never leave us! Yes – he has given us his Spirit so that we might always know his presence! *But he doesn't want us hiding in the comfort and security of just hanging out with the church crowd!* With the promise that he will be with us wherever we go, Jesus wants us *out there in dangerous territory,* telling the story of what he has done for us. Look at what he tells this transformed man:

> **Mark 5:19** *"Jesus did not let him, but said, 'Go home to your family and tell them how much the Lord has done for you, and how he has had mercy on you'."*

Every disciple has a story to tell. You simply explain to others what the Lord has done for you. So help the new disciple tell their story. Share your story of Jesus with them. Full instructions for helping a new believer share their story are given in *"Discipleship Training – Book 1: Study 4"* – but here is a summary of how to help a new believer tell their story:

- *Divide your story into 3 sections:*
    - o *Before I trusted Christ*
    - o *How I trusted Christ*
    - o *Since I've trusted Christ*
- *Keep it brief: no more than 1 minute on each section.*
- *Keep it personal.*
- *Keep Jesus central: it's a story of what he has done for you.*
- *Use God's word: include one Bible verse in your story.*
- *Finish with a challenge.*

Help new believers to tell their story. It will not only reinforce what Jesus has done for them, but they will start to discover what Jesus can do for others!

7. Get them bringing others

The simplest way for a new believer to reach others for Jesus is to bring them to Christian events where their friends can find out about Jesus. Train them to be champion bringers: bring their friends to church. bring their friends to your youth group. bring their friends to your small group.

Can you notice that I suggested that they *bring* their friends, not merely *invite* them? Both are good – but there is a difference. *Inviting* merely means that having issued the invitation, you wait and see whether they will indeed show up. *Bringing* means that in addition to inviting your friends, you then make arrangements to *bring* them with you. Offer transport. Pick them up. Have coffee together first. *Bringing* is exponentially more effective than merely *inviting!*

8. Witness with them

The whole principle of *discipling by imitation* is that the new believer will learn how to minister by watching you. So, when new friends are brought to church, you show the new believer how to talk to them about Jesus by doing it yourself. Have them watch. Have them pray. Invite them to join in. Invite them to tell their story.

If you're involved in a more informal outreach setting (e.g. inviting some unsaved friends to your home for dinner), then have your new believers come as well. They will learn from you how they too can have a powerful ministry with unbelievers.

If you're working with students, help them to organise a "thank-you dinner" to honour their parents. Invite all the parents – both Christian and non-Christian – to someone's home for dinner, and help your students do all the preparation and catering. It is an opportunity for them to serve their parents and honour them. During the course of the evening, have a number of the students share their testimonies! This could be a great outreach to their parents!

And of course, you're not just trying to model how to share your faith in Jesus; you're trying to show the new disciple *how they will be able to train someone else!* So talk about the witnessing opportunity before it happens; pray together for your unsaved friends; and after the event, talk through everything that happened and plan for future outreach opportunities.

9. Serve with them

A great way to establish life-long habits of active ministry is to look for ways to serve alongside the new believers. Help them to see that ministry often involves rolling your sleeves up and serving in practical ways. There is a world out there that needs the love of Jesus – and, following his encouragement, we know that as we serve others, we are serving Jesus himself.

> **Matthew 25:40** *"The King will reply, 'I tell you the truth, whatever you did for one of the least of these brothers of mine, you did for me'."*

Is there a way that you can join with the new disciples and serve your community with the love of Christ?

- Join in helping in a community project.

- Serve together in a soup kitchen.

- Visit the elderly together in a retirement village.

- Deliver meals to those in need.

- Experience a short-term mission placement together.

- Do maintenance and repairs at a struggling church.

There is no end to the possibilities, but do not neglect this part of a disciple's training for ministry. Jump in with them – work together on something worthwhile – and enjoy seeing the difference that you can make to the lives of others.

Over the decades, my observation is that getting new believers involved in frontline ministries *from the word go* is one of the keys to transforming them into world-changing disciples.

Chapter 19

Memorising verses

I have had the privilege of discipling many young people. I have had the joy of watching many of them go on to Christian maturity and stand strongly for Jesus in their day-to-day life. I have the satisfaction of seeing many of those in active gospel ministry at their local church. Here is an observation from watching generations of disciples go on in their faith and ministry: *those who memorised Bible verses have an extra weapon in their arsenal as they seek to stand for Jesus in this world.* There is no command in the Bible that says you have to memorise verses – and in these modern educational days *learning by rote* is probably not valued as much as it once was – but in my own life as a Christian, and in the lives of so many whom I have discipled, knowing Bible verses *by heart* has proved to be a most indispensable asset.

I never quite know where people get these statistics from, but I have heard that most people who only hear God's word will remember about 5%; combine reading with hearing and you'll remember about 15%; and then by studying God's word you will increase your retention to about 35%. Whatever the basis of these figures, here is one figure which is indisputable: *when you memorise a verse by heart, you remember 100% of it!*

1. The benefits of memory verses

Here are some biblical reasons why many Christians have found memorising God's word so helpful:

a) It helps you focus on God

> **Psalm 1:2** *"But his delight is in the law of the LORD, and on his law he meditates day and night."*

God wants us to have a real love for his word and for it to be with us constantly. When you memorise sections of God's word, you really will be able to meditate on it 'day and night'.

b) It helps you guard against sin

> **Psalm 119:11** *"I have hidden your word in my heart that I might not sin against you."*

When you know God's word, you can rely on that in times of temptation to help you from giving in to sin. When Jesus was resisting the temptations of Satan in the wilderness *(Matthew 4:3-4)*, he used his knowledge of Scripture to fend off the devil's attacks. When you memorise specific verses, you can use them to guard your heart. Rather than trusting in the lie that Satan is telling you, you can know *for certain* what God has said on the same issue.

c) It helps you minister to others

> **Colossians 3:16** *"Let the word of Christ dwell in you richly as you teach and admonish one another with all wisdom."*

When you know what God's word is on specific topics, you can use that verse to help someone else. Rather than relying on what you *think* God might have said, you can minister with confidence because you *know* what God has said.

I was sitting with my Year 10 boys in our discipleship group. The topic came around to *dealing with temptation*. Some of the boys were having a bit of a struggle.

Mike had a question he wanted to ask. *"What do you do when you're faced with a temptation that is just too hard?"* I asked the others what they thought, and they all agreed that there were temptations that were too difficult to overcome. There were situations they all faced where they felt they had no other choice but to give in to sin.

As the conversation continued, I asked, *"Can you think of anything God has said that would help you to have **victory over sin**?"* (I chose those last three words carefully, as they form the heading for one of the verses we had memorised.)

"There's that verse we learnt!" chipped in John. *"What did it say again?"*

The boys knew the verse *(1 Corinthians 10:13)*. They said it from memory until we got to the part where it says *"he will not let you be tempted beyond what you can bear"*. So I asked the question: *"Is there ever a temptation that is **really** too hard to resist?"* The boys could see that even though certain temptations *felt* as if they were too strong, they had a memory verse where God specifically promised that temptation will *never* be too strong.

Knowing this verse helped them to answer their own question. Rather than thinking they *had* to give in to certain temptations, they decided to pursue the strategy in the verse: *"But when you are tempted, he will also provide a way out so that you can stand up under it"*. Rather than feeling they *had* to give in, they started looking for the *way out* that God had promised to provide.

2. How to teach memory verses

- *Learn the verse yourself before you set the task to the students. Make sure you know it "word perfectly". Show your students that it's not an onerous task!*

- *Drill your students in the* **formula** *for learning a verse. If you keep this consistent across every verse, it makes it easier to remember them all. Here is the 4-step formula:*

1	The heading	e.g. *New Life in Christ*
2	The reference	e.g. *2 Corinthians 5:17*
3	The full verse	*Therefore, if anyone is in Christ, he is a new creation; the old has gone, the new has come!*
4	Repeat the reference	e.g. *2 Corinthians 5:17*

- *After you have demonstrated how to learn the verse, set the students the task of memorising the verse* **word-perfectly** *before your group meets the next week. You might even want to teach the first verse to everyone while they're at your group!*

- *To help them memorise it easily, teach them this method:*

1	Memorise the heading. Say it over a few times to make sure you have it.
2	Then add the reference. Say the reference over a few times to make sure you have it.
3	Then put the two together. Say, from memory, the heading followed by the reference.
4	Continue this method to add the whole verse. Memorise the first short phrase of the verse; then when you know you've got it right, try and run the whole thing through from the beginning. Check any errors, and then add the next phrase.
5	Continue this until you have the **whole verse** memorised, including the heading and reference at the beginning, and the reference repeated at the end.
6	Then write out the whole verse from memory. Then check it word for word with the original, to make sure you have no errors. Repeat this process until you have the whole thing **word perfect.**

- *This whole process should take about 5 minutes for the average verse.* **But it's really important to do this early in the week, so you're able to reinforce it in your memory using the following technique.** *Otherwise, the verse won't "stick".*

  - Once you have memorised the verse perfectly, run it through your head three times in the next hour.

- Then run it through your head three times during the rest of the day.

- Then run it through your head once a day for the rest of the week.

- *The first week you set a memory verse, contact each student individually during the week to make sure that they know it.* **This is vital to do for the first memory verse!** *You need to set a standard in your group that 'everyone knows it'.*

- *When you meet the following week, have every person in your group say the verse from memory (you start!). Encourage those who are faltering, but maintain the standard of having it word perfect. Celebrate when the whole group succeeds!*

I know that memorising verses is hard work. I know that sometimes you will find it difficult to discipline yourself to get your memory work done. Certainly your young people will find it tricky sometimes – and may even complain that you make them do it!

But when I catch up with those whom I have discipled – those who are now powering on in the faith as a result of the hard work we put in when they were younger – not one of them has ever regretted memorising verses from the Bible. Indeed many have thanked me for it. Many still use those same verses decades after they first memorised them.

If there is one thing you could add to your discipleship training that would lift you to *another level,* I would never hesitate to introduce memory verses. For a small investment of time – and a small amount of hard work now – they will reap rich dividends for a lifetime.

Chapter 20

Trusting God

One of the biggest dangers in having an effective discipling method in your local church is that you can end up trusting your discipleship method to produce the results.

*"What do you mean? I thought the whole idea of having a good discipling programme was that it **would** produce results for you?"*

There's the problem in a nutshell. This whole book has argued for an intentional strategy to train disciples that they might stand faithfully for Jesus and be passionate to make other disciples in this world. I want to encourage churches to set up methods and programmes so that they will in fact achieve the one thing that Jesus wants them to achieve – to *"make disciples of all nations"*. In my own church I have laboured hard to change the programme so that it intentionally has a sharper discipleship focus.

*But it is not the programme that will raise up faithful and mighty disciples. It is the power of God **and nothing else!***

I was chatting with the pastor of a large and growing church. He was reflecting on his emphasis on disciple-making. They had a great system – a very well thought-through programme. They had an extensive small-group network – they trained their leaders well – they held their disciples accountable for their growth – everything was tracked tightly – and their follow-up process was second to none.

With a look of despair in his eyes and a mischievous grin on his lips, this pastor said to me: *"You know, I sometimes worry that our discipleship programme is so good, it's almost like we don't need God any more."*

I understood what he meant. The danger of having a great ministry programme is that we can end up thinking that it's *our great programme* that makes the whole thing happen. It never is. If great things are happening in our churches, it is because God himself is making it happen. And if our programmes are *so slick* that we almost feel like we don't *need* God anymore, then our ministry and our lives are in dangerous territory.

In my experience, *bad* discipleship programmes go off the rails because they are simply not thought through well enough. There is no intentionality; there is no accountability; there is no vision for an end result. On the other hand, *good* discipleship programmes can go off the rails *because the programme is so good, that 'depending on God' gets squeezed out.* And no discipleship system – no matter how *good,* no matter how *tight,* no matter how *well organised* – will ever produce lasting disciples of its own accord. No programme on earth is powerful enough *in its own strength* to transform new believers into world-changing disciples.

Recently, I was reading from the prophet Jeremiah. Jeremiah found himself in a difficult situation. The people of Israel had given up trusting in God, and were now basing their hope on the fact that they were the *people of God.* They were God's nation; they were God's people; they occupied God's land; they worshipped in God's temple. Surely with all this going for them they could rely on always experiencing God's blessings. Couldn't they?

But the message of Jeremiah isn't a message that *"everything will be okay"*. Jeremiah brings a message that, because God's people had given up on trusting God, He was going to hand them over to their enemies and allow them to be overtaken by the unbelieving nation of Babylon.

As I read through Jeremiah's message, I saw a clear warning against trusting in a mere ministry programme to produce results.

1. Trusting in yourself

a) The problem of trusting in your own ideas

> ***Jeremiah 17:5*** *"This is what the LORD says: 'Cursed is the one who trusts in man, who depends on flesh for his strength and whose heart turns away from the LORD.'"*

What's the big deal with having confidence in my own abilities? Why can't I simply know that my own strengths are good enough to get us through? Here's the problem: *as soon as I place more trust in myself, I place less trust in God.* It's all got to do with where my heart is.

This has been the perennial problem for God's people. Here's the way it goes time and time again in the pages of scripture:

> *i. God's people have nothing.*
> *ii. They trust God for everything.*
> *iii. God gives them everything.*
> *iv. They now trust God for nothing.*
> *v. They end up with nothing.*

Here's the way it sometimes works in my own ministry:

i.   *I desperately want a fruitful ministry – I don't know how to do it – I have no resources – I have no ideas – I have nothing.*

ii. *I cry out to God in prayer, knowing that he alone can make this happen.*

iii. *God hears my prayer – he provides the resources – he provides the ideas – he provides a fruitful, growing ministry.*

iv. *I develop this ministry – refine it – systematise it – strategise it – write books about it – establish it as an ongoing enterprise – feel confident in it.*

v.   *I end up trusting the ministry system – not trusting God – and wonder why we're not getting the results that we used to.*

Have you ever fallen into that trap? It can be so easy to trust in what God gives us, rather than trusting in the God who has given all to us. I've seen this happen so many times in discipling ministries. You develop a system for training disciples; it's a *good* system – it's an *effective* system – it's a *godly* system – in fact, the system is so good that you end up trusting *it* rather than trusting God.

It's easy to determine whether you've fallen into this trap: *check the results you're getting!*

b) The result of trusting in your own ideas

> **Jeremiah 17:6** *"He will be like a bush in the wastelands; he will not see prosperity when it comes. He will dwell in the parched places of the desert, in a salt land where no one lives."*

If you know the Australian outback, then you can vividly picture what God is talking about. If you've driven in the far-flung country areas, you will instantly recognise the dry scrub that exists on the fringe of the desert. There are small pockets of sparse vegetation on the edge of the salt lake. Everything is dry. Everything is barren. Everything is fighting for its very survival.

Have you ever felt like that in ministry? Maybe you are trying so hard to disciple others that you yourself feel burnt out. You're committed to your ministry – in one sense you *love* your ministry. But it's simply wearing you out. It's not as much fun as it used to be. It feels dry. It feels barren. It feels routine. It feels as if you're just churning your way through the programme one more time.

Can you imagine the effect this has on the young people whom you're discipling? They might look on-fire as Christians; they might be forging ahead as disciples; but maybe they too are just getting into a rut and missing the genuine refreshment that Jesus offers.

I've seen it happen. Young people who work *so hard* at being disciples that they just run themselves into the ground. Keen Christians who plug into a thorough and unrelenting ministry programme with demanding standards. I've seen keen Christians burnt out in their desire to grow into faithful disciples.

Sean was one of our keen young Christian men. Just out of high school, he was on the verge of making decisions that would affect the whole of his life. He was growing strongly as God's son – keen to be a faithful disciple.

His family moved away and he moved along with

them. It was great to hear that he had plugged into a local church and that he was actively involved in being trained as a disciple. He would send me glowing reports of his great new church and keep me informed about the leaps and bounds he was making in his personal walk with Jesus.

A few months on, his reports were less enthusiastic. He loved the challenge of his church's rigorous discipleship scheme; he was so keen to do it well; but he found that the programme was unrelenting and unforgiving. No matter how hard he tried, he felt he could never live up to what was expected of him.

They met for Bible study and prayer each Wednesday at 6am. They had large memory verses each week. A stack of "homework" to be done. If they hadn't completed their work, they weren't allowed to take part in discussion in their group. They had rigorous ministry assignments, and they appeared to be busy every day of the week. On paper the programme looked good. But I feared that the programme had become all important and that God wasn't getting much of a look-in. With the best will in the world, young Sean was simply being *burnt out* as he struggled to become the man that he thought God wanted him to be. He was fitting the description of Jeremiah 17:6

Jeremiah 17:6 *"He will be like a bush in the wastelands; he will not see prosperity when it comes. He will dwell in the parched places of the desert, in a salt land where no one lives."*

Contrast this with the rich refreshment which is found in truly trusting God!

2. Trusting in God

a) The joy of trusting in God

> **Jeremiah 17:7** *"But blessed is the man who trusts in the LORD, whose confidence is in him."*

God does not essentially call people to a programme; he does not primarily call them to a ministry; he doesn't even chiefly call them to a church or Christian organisation; *he firstly calls them to himself.* He wants to refresh and enliven every believer. He wants an intimacy that nurtures a deeply loving relationship. He wants a vital union, where each one of us is supported by the strength and power that God alone can give.

I need to remember this about my own ministry. Before I get all *gung-ho* about plunging the world into yet another ministry programme, I need to understand that God wants *me.* Before he wants my gifts, before he wants my ideas, before he wants my ministry – he wants me. He wants to refresh me. He wants to forgive me. He wants to hold me as his own. He wants to love me.

That's also what he wants from those whom I disciple. Sure, he wants to use me to draw others to him – but he doesn't want me getting in the way. He is not calling his disciples to a programme – he is calling them to a relationship.

If I want to see fruitful growth from my discipleship ministry at my church, then I need to be aware that God first wants to see fruitful growth in my heart. Because it's what's in my heart that will be reproduced into the hearts of those whom I lead.

b) The results of trusting in God

When I sink my roots deeply into God, and draw on the refreshment that he supplies, then I reap all the benefits of being a well-watered tree. And what are those benefits?

i You will not burn out

> **Jeremiah 17:8** *"He will be like a tree planted by the water that sends out its roots by the stream. **It does not fear when heat comes** ... **It has no worries in a year of drought.**"*

A plant that is under-watered is in real trouble when the heatwave comes. But a tree that is planted by the water, that sends its roots by the stream *does not fear when heat comes; it has no worries in a year of drought.*

That's the vision we must have for those we are discipling! If we have worked with them; helped them have a real desire to immerse themselves into God's loving arms; encouraged them to soak in the refreshment of God's word and prayer; and helped them be planted by running streams – then we are preparing them for the day when the heat comes. When their Christian life is under pressure – when their discipleship is under attack – they will not burn out. They will be well-watered.

ii You will be fruitful

> **Jeremiah 17:8** *"its leaves are always green ... [it] never fails to bear fruit"*

Our aim in training disciples is that they will be fruitful. Fruitful in their own growth for Jesus; fruitful in their ministry. Fruitful for a lifetime; fruitful long after we are forgotten. If we can have a ministry that steers away from the sin of *trusting our own programmes and ideas,* and focuses squarely on *trusting God to achieve the results,* then we can enjoy the refreshment and joy that God himself will bring.

Now, check out what the *key influencing factor* is in determining what sort of ministry we will end up with!

3. Checking my heart

a) The problem of trusting my own heart

> ***Jeremiah 17:9*** *"The heart is deceitful above all things and beyond cure. Who can understand it?"*

The single most important factor that will have the biggest influence over the sort of discipling ministry that I have is this: *it is the state of my heart.* For it's what's in my heart that will be reproduced in those whom I lead.

The scary thing about the verse in Jeremiah is this: *my heart can change at a moment's notice!* It is not to be trusted! Sometimes at my point of *deepest devotion*, my heart will respond with the most *wilful rebellion.*

- *When God is blessing our ministry the most, I find I am at my easiest moment to start feeling wrongfully proud and taking the glory for myself.*

- *I know a pastor, who when sitting at his computer preparing a sermon, finds that right then is the time he is most likely to visit pornographic websites.*

- *A friend of mine worked on a Christian camp and did the most magnificent job in helping many students turn to Jesus. The week he returned home he was almost at the point of giving up on his own faith.*

- *One of our most outstanding discipleship leaders had an area of personal disobedience which he kept hidden for ages. By the time we discovered it, that area of disobedience had been copied by those whom he led.*

Here's the problem: *just when you think you can trust your own heart, you will find that it lets you – and God – down!* That's why it matters to be planted by streams of water so that you will not wither when the heat comes!

b) The solution to trusting my own heart

Jeremiah 17:10 "I the LORD search the heart and examine the mind, to reward a man according to his conduct, according to what his deeds deserve."

God is making a very simple observation in this verse: everything we do has consequences. It is God who searches our hearts and examines our minds. Nothing will escape him. Our only hope is that he will cleanse our hearts and purify our minds. That's why Jesus came – to deal with our sin and purify us for God.

Our only solution is to cry out to God and beg him to deal with our unpredictable hearts:

Psalm 139:23-24 "Search me, O God, and know my heart; test me and know my anxious thoughts. See if there is any offensive way in me, and lead me in the way everlasting."

To my mind, that is the final "missing link" in discipleship.

It is the ultimate danger. That we turn discipleship into a human educational experience, rather than an encounter with the living God. That discipleship gets reduced to a curriculum rather than an immersion into God himself. That we let our hearts go uncontrolled and unchecked, and end up with a ministry where we have fashioned our own disciples after our own image.

God has made us in his image. By reflecting that image, we get to shape and mould other disciples so that they too will live in God's image. And we teach and grow them in such a way that they are equipped to go and reach many others. From one generation to the next. And by doing this we get to accomplish the one job that Jesus has left for us here on planet earth: *to make disciples of all nations!*

Let's do it!

SECTION 6

Appendixes

Appendix 1 – Discipleship Training Outline

*This is the complete outline of all the studies contained within the 5 books of the "Discipleship Training" series. When I wrote these studies, the question I was trying to tackle was this: "If I had some young disciples for a few years – and I needed to ground them in all the basics of discipleship so that they could go on and live as lifelong, passionate and faithful disciples, **what would I teach them?**"*

The following is the result. It took me four years to write and it has been fine-tuned over the past two decades. I trust it is a huge blessing for you as you go about your challenge of "making disciples of all nations"!

Book 1 – My New Life

This reinforces the step of faith that a new Christian has taken, and covers the fundamentals of being a faithful disciple and a passionate disciple-maker.

1.1   I'm a disciple

This looks at the intimate relationship described in John 15 of being a branch that is organically united to the vine. This is to introduce the new disciple to their ongoing relationship with Jesus.

1.2   I'm a disciple-maker

This introduces the new disciple to their mission of making disciples of others. The concept of being a "witness" is investigated further in Book 4.

1.3 I'm praying for my friends
This introduces the new disciple to the simple yet powerful ministry of regularly praying for three unsaved friends.

1.4 I'm sharing my faith
This helps the new disciple to share their story of the difference that Jesus has made to their life.

1.5 I'm trusting Christ's power
This helps the new disciple to understand the blessings and riches that they have in Christ. This is to help them trust in Christ's strength, rather then trying to achieve everything by their own abilities.

1.6 I'm safe in God's hands
This is to reassure the new disciple that it's not just up to them to hang in as a Christian. If they have truly made a decision to follow Jesus, then God has them safely in his hand and will hang on to them no matter what.

1.7 I'm spending time with God
This is to ground the new disciple in regular personal time with God. This introduces the topics of Bible reading and prayer,which are investigated further in Book 3.

1.8 I'm dealing with my sin
This is to help the new disciple experience victory in dealing with temptation. This introduces the topic of obedience, which is investigated in more detail in Book 5.

1.9 I'm part of God's family
This is to establish the new disciple in the regular habit of

meeting with other Christians – both in their small group, and at church. It introduces the concept of encouraging other Christians, which is further explored in Book 4.

1.10   Instant replay
This study reviews all the topics and memory verses from Book 1.

Book 2 – My Awesome God
This introduces the growing disciple to the magnificence and intimacy of God, who reveals himself as Father, Son and Holy Spirit.

2.1   The one and only
This explores Isaiah 40:12-31 and shows the magnificence and majesty of God who rules over heaven and earth. There is no-one like him!

2.2   God is my Father
This shows the intimacy and care of God as our heavenly Father.

2.3   The promised Messiah
This introduces us to the Old Testament prophecies that predict the coming of Jesus. This shows us that Jesus is fully God – from all eternity.

2.4 The Servant King

Explores Philippians 2: 5-11 to show the magnificence of Jesus' death and resurrection and what they mean for us.

2.5 The returning Lord

This introduces the teaching that Jesus will return one day as lord to judge to the living and the dead.

2.6 God's Spirit lives in me

Assures us that God's Holy Spirit lives in every believer. He is a great gift from God to help and guide us, and to assure us that we really belong to God.

2.7 God's Spirit changes me

This shows us that one of the major works of the Holy Spirit is to change us to be more and more like Jesus. If we're open to the Spirit's leading, we will produce the fruit of the Spirit.

2.8 God's Spirit equips me

This shows the other major work of the Spirit – to equip us for ministry. We are urged to stay in step with the Spirit so that we will live the way God wants us to. (Spiritual gifts are discussed later in Book 4.)

2.9 Instant replay

This study reviews all the topics and memory verses from Book 2.

Book 3 – My Intimate Relationship

These studies focus on two key areas: to learn to listen to God as he speaks through his word, and to grow in confidence to bring everything before God in prayer.

3.1 Hear and read God's word

Introduces us to the importance of God's word, and the need to keep hearing it and reading it.

3.2 Study and memorise God's word

Shows the added benefit of firstly studying God's word, and then memorising sections of it.

3.3 Meditate on God's word

Introduces the concept of meditating on God's word – of visualising it – expressing it in you own words – applying it – and immersing yourself in it.

3.4 Obey God's word

Shows that God's word is not just something to be read – it is something to be lived out. A very practical study!

3.5 The importance of prayer

Introduces the growing disciple to the place of prayer in their life. Shows how vital it is to retain an intimate relationship with God.

3.6 Does God answer my prayers?

Investigates the promises of God to hear and answer prayer. Helps disciples understand the situations where God's answer is different from what we'd hoped for.

3.7 How should I pray?

Investigates different styles of prayer to give the growing disciple a balanced prayer life. Teaches us to pray four sorts of prayer: *"I love you"*, *"Sorry"*, *"Thanks"* and *"Please"*.

3.8 Enjoying God in praise

Introduces us to praise as a crucial form of prayer. Helps us to have a genuine experience of biblical praise.

3.9 Praying biblically

Introduces us to some of the great prayers of the Bible, and teaches how to pray in a similar way.

3.10 Instant replay

This study reviews all the topics and memory verses from Book 3.

Book 4 – My Mission From God

Introduces us to the two key aspects of every disciple's mission: to be a faithful manager (steward) of all God has given us, and to be a witness for Christ in our dying world.

4.1 I'm a witness for Christ

Introduces us to the ministry of sharing our faith with our non-Christian friends.

4.2 I've got the power of the gospel

Encourages us to be bold as witnesses because we have a powerful message – a gospel from God that has the power to transform lives.

4.3   I've got the power of love

Shows that spreading the gospel is not just about words – but about actions. Helps us to put genuine Christlike love into practice.

4.4   I can grow other disciples

Introduces us to the ministry of training another disciple. This will give us the confidence to "follow up" another new believer.

4.5   I can impact the world

This is aimed at enlarging our vision to see that *the whole world* needs to be brought to Christ. Shows us the starting point for having a world-wide impact.

4.6   God has put me in charge

This introduces the mission of being a *steward* or a *manager*. God has entrusted us with many things, and our job is to use all those things to extend God's kingdom and bless others.

4.7   I'm a steward of God's ministry gifts

Introduces *spiritual gifts* and shows us how we're meant to use them to serve and build up others. Helps the group to identify each other's gifts – and encourage each other to use them well.

4.8   I'm a steward of God's time

Helps us to compare God's priorities with our priorities (as evidenced by our use of time). A simple way to help us instigate godly time management.

4.9 I'm a steward of God's money

Introduces us to the principle of being generous, and our understanding of *tithe*. Challenges disciples to be super-generous with their money and possessions. Helps them start a simple giving plan.

4.10 Instant replay

This study reviews all the topics and memory verses from Book 4.

Book 5 – My Personal Obedience

Helps us to understand what it means to treat Jesus as Lord – in every area of our life. Tackles some obedience issues which are often stumbling blocks for young disciples.

5.1 How to treat Jesus as Lord

Shows how Jesus is Lord over absolutely everything – and how we need to submit to that lordship in every area of our life.

5.2 How to really trust God

Helps the growing disciple to live life by faith and not by sight. Helps us to learn how to trust God's promises.

5.3 How to live a new life

Investigates Ephesians Chs 4-6 to highlight all the implications of living a new life.

5.4 How to make godly decisions

Shows how God's promises are trustworthy, and his guidance is sure. Helps growing disciples to make wise decisions based on biblical principles.

5.5 My speech

Helps us to understand the power of the tongue, and to learn to speak words of life.

5.6 My submission

Introduces *submission* as a way of life for a Christian, and shows young people how to be joyfully submissive to their parents.

5.7 Study

Shows the biblical thinking to help us make wise decisions about our study life. Encourages students to avoid the excesses of both laziness and over-commitment to studying.

5.8 Alcohol

Shows how alcohol is a gift from God to bless us, but how its abuse leads to so much destruction. Investigates the biblical factors in making a personal decision.

5.9 Being in love

Helps us to understand the biblical concept of love, and shows us how to apply it to a romantic relationship.

5:10 Sex

Shows the biblical teaching about sexuality, which sees it as a beautiful gift from God given for our enjoyment. But we also see the danger of using this great gift outside of God's guidelines. A call to purity!

5.11 Instant replay

This study reviews all the topics and memory verses from Book 5.

Appendix 2 - Growing Young Disciples Outline

Discipleship for 11-14s

This is a shortened discipling course which is particularly designed for junior highs. All these studies are contained in the 5 books of the "Growing Young Disciples" Series. The aim of these studies is to establish pre-teens in the absolute basics of living as disciples of Jesus.

Book 1 – Discovering Jesus

This takes the new believer through the steps of the gospel to help them know for certain whether they are truly saved.

1.1   Discovering God

Introduces the student to the character of God.   In particular, that God cannot stand our sin.

1.2   Discovering me

As well as showing how precious we are to God, this study shows that all of us sin; all of us are in rebellion against God; all of us deserve God's punishment.   Raises the question: *If all of us deserve God's punishment – how can any of us every make it to heaven?*

1.3   Discovering Jesus

Introduces Jesus and shows how he is both fully God and fully human. And yet amazingly, Jesus never sinned. He is the only one who does not deserve any punishment from God; the only one who deserves to make it to heaven.

1.4   Discovering Jesus' death

Shows clearly how Jesus takes our sins so that we can be forgiven. Goes step by step through the gospel, and challenges students to think through whether **they** are truly forgiven or not.

1.5   Discovering my response

Shows clearly that a response is demanded of each person – shows what that response is – and helps students to work out whether they are ready to make it.

Book 2 – First Steps

These studies take the new disciple through the basic steps of discipleship – fellowship, the Bible, prayer and obedience.

2.1   What's happened to me?

This is a refresher course to highlight the changes that happen when you give your life to Jesus.

2.2   You're in the family

Welcomes the new believer to the blessings of gathering with God's people – in church, and in your Bible-study group.

2.3   Let's listen to God

Establishes the new believer in the discipleship habit of regular Bible reading.

2.4   Let's talk with God

Establishes the new believer in the discipleship habit of regular prayer.

2.5 A new way to live

Highlights the importance of being able to see specific life-change now that you are a follower of Jesus.

Book 3 – Life to the max

These studies are designed to help 11-14s live faith-filled lives. Not just to coast along trusting in their own strength – but to actively seek to be Christlike in all that they say or do. These studies show that there's only one way to live for Jesus – flat out!

3.1 Life to the max – by trusting Jesus

This study is to show students what faith really is – and to help them to live faith-filled lives.

3.2 Life to the max – by overcoming temptation

This study is to help students deal with the temptations in their lives, and enjoy living for Jesus by dealing with their sin.

3.3 Life to the max – by loving like God does

This shows us how fantastically loving God is – and challenges us to live our lives with the same sort of love.

3.4 Life to the max – by forgiving like God does

This shows us how fantastically forgiving God is – and challenges us to live our lives with the same sort of forgiveness.

3.5 Life to the max – by giving like God does

This shows us how fantastically generous God is – and challenges us to live our lives with the same sort of generosity.

Book 4 – Dealing With Doubt

This book is designed to help junior highs deal with the issue of doubt. *For any young Christian, there will often be nagging questions:* "Am I really a Christian? How do I know I'm really forgiven? Has God given up on me?" *These five studies will help junior highs to work through these doubts, and to understand the promises that God has made in his word, and the power that God has given them to help them live for him.*

4.1   Has God really accepted me?
Helps clear up the biggest doubt that new Christians often have: *"Am I really a Christian, or am I just pretending?"* This study is to help students to know for sure that if they are serious about following Jesus, God is serious about hanging on to them.

4.2   Has God really forgiven me?
It's very easy to feel guilty because of your sin. Sometimes we can *know* about God's forgiveness without really *experiencing* it. This study looks at four facts to help us see how total and absolute God's forgiveness really is. Then we can live as people who are *truly forgiven.*

4.3   Does God really love me?
"I know God is loving. But how could he love me?" This study aims to show junior highs that God's love is bigger than they can ever imagine, and that they can trust him to love them no matter what.

4.4   Is God really changing me?
It can be really encouraging as a Christian if you can see the *progress* God is making in your life. This study is to assure young people of the *presence* of God's Holy Spirit

in their life, and for them to experience the *power* of God's Holy Spirit in their ongoing growth.

4.5 Can God really use me?

In God's master plan to *make disciples of all nations,* he wants to use you! This study shows students how God has both called them and equipped them so that they can help their friends to discover Jesus. A great introduction to witnessing for Christ.

Book 5 – Sticking With It

These studies work through Peter's first letter – which is written to new Christians. It is ideal material for those who are young in their faith to work through. It covers an array of topics that are extremely useful to those in their early days of their spiritual journey. These studies are meant to be genuine encouragements for students who probably sometimes feel like giving up.

5.1 Sometimes it's really difficult
1 Peter 1:1-12

Introduces the whole letter – reminds us of what God has done for us – and gives practical advice on how to keep going when it gets tough.

5.2 Do I really have to change my life?
1 Peter 1:13 – 2:3

Looks at the big changes that God has planned for those who follow him, reminds us of the price that God has paid to take us back, and gives down-to-earth advice on living for Jesus.

5.3 What difference does Jesus make?
1 Peter 2:4-10

A great study to focus on who Jesus is, and what it means to be gathered around him as his people.

5.4 Can't I just do what I like?
1 Peter 2:11-25

What does it mean to be free in Christ? This study shows how Jesus sacrificed himself as a servant, and now calls on us to serve others in the same way.

5.5 But I want to have a good time!
1 Peter 3: 1-12

Looks at the biblical principles behind boy/girl relationships – and the Bible's guide to having a "good time"!

5.6 What if my friends don't believe?
1 Peter 3:13 – 4:6

Helps junior highs to stand up for Jesus with their non-Christian friends.

5.7 You mean I can help others?
1 Peter 4:7-19

Helps junior highs to identify and use their spiritual gifts, and to stand strong for Jesus when others are pushing them down.

5.8 Sticking at it – together
1 Peter 5:1-14

Shows the importance of living for Jesus in the community of God's people (church) so that they can be strong against the devil's attacks.

Appendix 3 – Memory Verses

1. New life in Christ – 2 Corinthians 5:17
"Therefore, if anyone is in Christ, he is a new creation; the old has gone, the new has come!"

2. Fellowship together – Hebrews 10:25
"Let us not give up meeting together, as some are in the habit of doing, but let us encourage one another – and all the more as you see the Day approaching."

3. All Scripture – 2 Timothy 3:16-17
"All Scripture is God-breathed and is useful for teaching, rebuking, correcting and training in righteousness, so that the man of God may be thoroughly equipped for every good work."

4. God answers prayer – John 15:7
"If you remain in me and my words remain in you, ask whatever you wish, and it will be given you."

5. Obeying God's word – James 1:22
"Do not merely listen to the word, and so deceive yourselves. Do what it says."

6. Eternal life in Jesus – John 5:24
"I tell you the truth, whoever hears my word and believes him who sent me has eternal life and will not be condemned; he has crossed over from death to life."

7. Jesus forgives me – 1 John 1:9
"If we confess our sins, he is faithful and just and will forgive us our sins and purify us from all unrighteousness."

8. God loves me – Psalm 103:11
"For as high as the heavens are above the earth, so great is his love for those who fear him."

9. God's Spirit changes me – Romans 8:9

"You, however, are controlled not by the sinful nature but by the Spirit, if the Spirit of God lives in you. And if anyone does not have the Spirit of Christ, he does not belong to Christ."

10. Witnessing for Christ – 1 Peter 3:15

"But in your hearts set apart Christ as Lord. Always be prepared to give an answer to everyone who asks you to give the reason for the hope that you have. But do this with gentleness and respect."

11. Living by faith – Philippians 4:13

"I can do everything through (Christ) who gives me strength."

12. Victory over sin – 1 Corinthians 10:13

"No temptation has seized you except what is common to man. And God is faithful; he will not let you be tempted beyond what you can bear. But when you are tempted, he will also provide a way out so that you can stand up under it."

13. Let your light shine – Matthew 5:16

"… Let your light shine before men, that they may see your good deeds and praise your Father in heaven."

14. Forgiving each other – Ephesians 4:32

"Be kind and compassionate to one another, forgiving each other, just as in Christ God forgave you."

15. The cheerful giver – 2 Corinthians 9:7

"Each man should give what he has decided in his heart to give, not reluctantly or under compulsion, for God loves a cheerful giver."

Appendix 4 – Response Form

RESPONSE FORM
SECTION 1 – THE PERSON

Name

Address ....

Phone

Email

❏ primary   ❏ high school   ❏ tertiary

❏ worker   ❏ unemployed   ❏ other

School attended ....

Year at school ....

What main activities does this person already attend at our church?

....

....

SECTION 2 – WHAT HAPPENED

Please tick the box(es) that best describe your conversation. If possible, tick only one box. Write further details below.

a)   ❏   Became a Christian

b)   ❏   Wants to become a Christian, but hasn't yet

c)   ❏   Already a Christian – wants to recommit life

d)   ❏   Asking questions / discussing problems

e)   ❏   Came to support a friend

Details: ....

SECTION 3 – THE OCCASION

What activity or occasion prompted this person to talk with you? *(e.g. follow up after youth outreach, camp etc)*

SECTION 4 – IMMEDIATE FOLLOW UP

1. Did you give out any literature? Please give details

2. What "next step" have you planned with this person?

3. What ongoing follow up do you recommend?

❑ I will do this follow up myself

❑ Follow up to be done by someone else

Suggested person:

SECTION 5 – THE COUNSELLOR

Your Name

Address

Phone

Email

Today's Date

Appendix 5 – Record Book of Sin

1 *Hold out both your hands*	These 2 hands represent 2 people.
2 *Now hold out just your right hand*	This hand represents the first person – me. *(give your name)*
3 *Place a book on your hand to represent sin*	But I have a problem – I sin against God. This book will represent a list of all my sins.

My sin stops me from enjoying life with God. And God says my sin must be punished.

So if I do nothing about my sin, and I stand before God to be judged, and he has to make a decision about whether I get into heaven, what will he say? Why? *(Wait for anwer, and help if needed.)* |
| **4** *Take away your right hand with the book, and hold out your left hand* | This second hand represents Jesus.

He never sinned. Never deserved any punishment from God at all.

So if Jesus were to stand before God to be judged, and God had to make a decision as to whether he would get into heaven – what would God say?

(Wait for answer, and help if needed.) |
| **5** *Bring back your left hand with the book* | When Jesus dies on the cross he takes the sin from all those who will turn and follow him… |

6 	... and placed that sin on himself. He suffered the punishment – the hell – that I deserve for my sins.
	The Bible says **"All of us have gone astray; each one of us has turned to his own way, but God has laid on Jesus the sin of us all"** (Isaiah 53:6)
	So what did God see when he looked at Jesus dying on the cross ? (Look at left hand with book – wait for answer.)
Transfer the book from your right hand to your left	And whose sin? (Wait for answer.)
	So what does God now see when he looks at me?
	(Look at left hand with book – wait for answer.)
	So if I were to stand before God now – to be judged – and he had to decide whether I go to heaven, what would he say? Why?
	(Look at left hand with book – wait for answer.)
	And Jesus didn't stay dead – but rose from the grave and now rules with God his Father!
7  *Put the book down, and pick it up again, so as not to confuse this with Jesus*	That means there are only two sorts of people in the world. Which one of these best represents where you are at right now?

Appendix 6 – Bibliography

Tim Hawkins, *Fruit That Will Last* (Hawkins 1999)
The overall biblical strategy for programming your youth
ministry. The perfect companion to *Disciples Who Will Last.*

Tim Hawkins, *Leaders Who Will Last* (Hawkins 2002)
The overall biblical strategy for building faithful youth leaders.

Tim Hawkins, *Discipleship Training* (CEP 2003)
5 volumes of Bible studies designed to train disciples – aimed at
senior high / young adult. Leader's Guide also available.

Tim Hawkins, *Growing Young Disciples* (CEP 1992)
5 volumes of Bible studies designed to train disciples – aimed at
junior high. Leader's Guide also available.

Philip Jensen, *Two Ways to Live: the choice we all face*
(Matthias Media 1978)
A concise presentation of the gospel.

Leroy Eims, *The Lost Art of Disciple Making*
(Zondervan: NavPress 1978)
The book that first inspired me to a ministry of disciple making.

Robert E Coleman, *The Master Plan of Evangelism*
(Power Books 1963) The Classic!

Most of these titles are available from The Good Book Company:

In the UK: www.thegoodbook.co.uk
tel: 0845 225 0880; admin@thegoodbook.co.uk

In the USA & Canada: www.thegoodbook.com
admin@thegoodbook.com

In Australia: www.hawkinsministry.com
(+61 2) 9629 6595; info@hawkinsministry.com